RAISING RACHAEL

by
DONNA J. FLANERY

PublishAmerica
Baltimore

© 2010 by Donna J. Flanery.
All rights reserved. No part of this book may be reproduced, stored in a retrieval system or transmitted in any form or by any means without the prior written permission of the publishers, except by a reviewer who may quote brief passages in a review to be printed in a newspaper, magazine or journal.

First printing

PublishAmerica has allowed this work to remain exactly as the author intended, verbatim, without editorial input.

ISBN: 978-1-4489-7838-0 (softcover)
ISBN: 978-1-4489-5784-2 (hardcover)
PUBLISHED BY PUBLISHAMERICA, LLLP
www.publishamerica.com
Baltimore

Printed in the United States of America

Hey Shawn waz up Cool my best friend Rachel hodgE

This book is for Rachael
and all of those that continue to inspire us.

To Shawn,
Always strive to be your best.
Always,
Donna J. Harvey

To Michael
for showing me the true meaning of unconditional love and support. May our children experience this type of relationship in their lives.

Table of Contents

THE BEGINNING	7
THE EARLY YEARS	11
EARLY EDUCATION	20
HIGH SCHOOL	31
TRANSITION - FROM CHILDHOOD TO ADULTHOOD	44
RELATIVELY SPEAKING (PART 1)	58
CHANGE AND NEW BEGINNINGS	67
RELATIVELY SPEAKING (PART 2)	80
RELATIONSHIPS	89
HABITS, BEHAVIORS, AND OBSESSIONS	95
ACTIVITIES, RESPONSIBILITIES, AND RIGHTS	104
LIVING HER DREAMS	112
DEALING WITH BEHAVIORS	117
MAKING PLANS	123
ILLNESS AND DEATH	130
BEING VULNERABLE	138
SERVICES	144
HAPPY ENDINGS	153
COMMON Q&A	155
NATIONAL RESOURCES	167
STATE RESOURCES	170

THE BEGINNING

I do not think any mother would knowingly wish to have a child with a disability. As mothers, we dream of having a perfect child. We wish them to grow up and have a perfect life without any problems. I would never have chosen for my child to face life with a disability. However, as we all know, life does not always turn out that way that we have planned.

Already having a small child, being pregnant again so soon was not on my to-do list. I didn't wish to be a young mother that just kept having babies. We couldn't afford another baby and I wasn't much more than a child myself. All things supposedly happen for a reason, so I convinced myself that being pregnant again was just one of those things.

The pregnancy itself was uneventful. I didn't have a lot of morning sickness and I was very healthy. I was learning to cook at this time, so I spent some time experimenting with different recipes. I finally mastered how to properly fry chicken. With my increased appetite, this was a good thing. The only thing that I remember craving was oven-toasted bagels with butter. I can almost taste it as I sit here remembering. It was a pleasant time in my life.

I can't forget the day I went into labor. My husband was in the military, at that time, and it was payday. I was at the commissary shopping for groceries on base just like any other payday. I started having a few light contractions in the store. I didn't pay much attention to them because I had already experienced some false labor. I just decided to ignore them and go about my business. As I finished up the shopping and headed to the register to pay, the contractions started to become closer and stronger. I decided to hurry up and head towards my apartment, which was about twenty minutes away. I stomped on the gas every time I felt a contraction. I am sure that if someone were watching the car it would have looked rather funny. I would be driving at normal speed and then out of nowhere I would accelerate. I continued this driving pattern the entire way home.

I arrived home and my husband unloaded the groceries. I called the doctor's office and the nurse asked if I wanted to come in or go to the hospital. I chose to go to the office because I didn't want to go to the hospital with another false alarm. Then I decided to do something women do out of vanity. I wanted to shave my legs before I went, just in case. It didn't matter that I would not be able to get out of the tub by myself. I just had the urge to have freshly shaven legs. I would have polished my toes if I could have reached them.

My husband had to take our son to stay with the neighbors in the event this was the real thing. We arrived at the doctor's office and were taken back right away. The doctor examined me and told me that I was already four centimeters dilated. It was time to go to the hospital. The car that we drove was an older model and had a few issues. It was a white Ford Granada with an oil leak. My husband decided that we needed to stop and get fuel. I found it a bit odd that we needed to stop now. Not only did he put fuel in the car but he added a quart of oil. By this time, my labor was becoming more intense and I felt the need to be moving towards the hospital. He was driving slowly because when our son was born, I was in labor for over eighteen hours. I believe he thought that he could take his time. Eventually we did make it to the hospital. For me it seemed to play out in slow motion and minutes seemed like hours.

The nurses were ready for me and I was taken back to my room. I was nervous but excited at the same time. My husband was ready to settle in for the long wait ahead. It was mid-afternoon, so he decided to watch a soap opera. This was strange, since he didn't normally watch them, but it had been a bit of a strange day. He didn't get to see much more than the opening credits because our daughter was born less than thirty minutes after our arrival at the hospital. She wasted no time in coming into the world. She came in loud and screaming. The doctor and nurses examined her and everything seemed to be normal. They cleaned her up and put her in my arms. She appeared to be perfectly healthy. I named her Rachael.

It wasn't until the next day when the nurses noticed a problem. I had been trying to breastfeed her and she just wasn't having any luck with getting suction. They assured me that sometimes it just takes a little time and that I should just rest and try again later. Rachael wasn't too fussy and the nurses took her back to the nursery. Later, I was lying in the hospital bed and a nurse came in to talk to me. She told me that there was a problem with my daughter. Maybe I was just too young and naive to realize that my whole world had changed. I was only twenty at the time with an eighteen-month-old at home. I had no clue as to what I was facing, so I did not feel scared. I did, however, feel numb and empty. I do not even think I cried that day. As I look back now, I can see that it was for the best. I had no expectations. I just knew that I had a little girl who needed me and that I would do whatever was necessary to protect and care for her.

I called my husband and tried to tell him what was going on to the best of my ability. All that I could say about the situation was that our daughter had a problem that would need to be repaired by a surgeon. I couldn't explain what I didn't fully understand myself. I just hoped that when the doctor came in, he could give me a better understanding of the problem.

This is my story of raising a child with a disability. I want to share what I have learned through the years in the hopes that somewhere along the way, it may just help someone else facing a similar situation. I am not a perfect parent. I have made my share of mistakes along the way. My approach to raising my daughter has helped shape her into a very independent and self-sufficient individual with thoughts and dreams of her own. I want to share with others so that they may catch a glimpse of what is possible.

If you have a child with a disability, the dreams and plans that you had for your child before his or her birth may need to be altered somewhat. That doesn't mean that you have to give up all hope. Just because you have a child with a disability, doesn't mean that you shouldn't expect a fulfilling life for your child.

THE EARLY YEARS

    I thought I was suffering from the flu. I went to the doctor and that is how I found out that I was pregnant. That was the only complication that I experienced in an otherwise normal and healthy pregnancy. I was young and in good physical shape and my pregnancy was routine. Rachael's delivery was very easy. She appeared healthy in every way. She was a healthy pink and had ten fingers and ten toes. It wasn't until she was a day old that the doctor diagnosed her with a cleft palate. On the surface, everything appeared normal but she was missing her soft palate. The soft palate is the soft tissue that makes up the back part of the roof of the mouth. Rachael's did not completely form before she was born. The nurses noticed that she was having difficulties getting any suction when they were trying to feed her.

    We stayed at the hospital for a few extra days so that I could learn how to take care of her needs. I was shown how to feed her and how to suction her out when needed. The nurses also taught me how she needed to sleep and other techniques to help her.

    The first twenty-four hours after we left the hospital were awful. Rachael was not getting enough nourishment. Most of what she drank came back out her nose. Rachael did not sleep any that first day. This means that I didn't sleep either. It took a while for me to learn how to calm her and to understand the nuances of feeding her correctly. It had seemed much easier while we were at the hospital. I used a special bottle that looked like a plastic flask. It had an extra long and flexible red nipple. I had to hold her in a sitting position to feed her. This is not the ideal way of trying to feed a newborn. Eventually, I began to get better with practice and Rachael was able to get the nutrition that she needed. Once I became more comfortable and relaxed, Rachael sensed it and soothing her became easier.

It was at our first appointment that we learned that Rachael had *Pierre Robin Syndrome*. (It would later be changed from a syndrome to a sequence.) *Pierre Robin Sequence* is characterized by an unusually small lower jaw (micrognathia) and downward displacement of the tongue (glossoptosis). Some infants also have an abnormal opening in the roof of the mouth (cleft palate); both the soft and hard palate can be affected. There are many other physical and mental issues that can occur due to this sequence.

Rachael was scheduled for her first surgery in her sixth week. Initially, I thought that one surgery would fix everything. I had no idea until after the first visit with the surgeon that we would be in for a long process. I came to understand that Rachael's condition would take a lot of time to correct and that it would not be an overnight miracle. I was very scared because she was so tiny and the procedure seemed so invasive. The doctor would place a piece of molded plastic over her missing palate. It would be held in place by metal screws. I kept trying to figure out how they could do this procedure in such a small place. She only weighed about eight pounds.

Rachael had the surgery when she was just six weeks old. When she came back into the recovery room, her tongue was sutured to the side of her mouth. She looked so small and helpless lying there. I felt that somehow this was my fault. I knew that it wasn't, but as a parent, you always feel responsible when your children go through something that causes them pain. She recovered quickly from the surgery and went home after a few days. This would be the first of many surgeries to come.

There were still many feeding issues after the initial surgery. For example, eighty to ninety percent of everything she ate came back out either through her mouth or her nose. I always had to be careful to make sure her airway stayed clear. Many times I had to turn her upside down and suction out her nose and mouth. I wasn't aware of any different way, so this seemed normal to me. After some time, it didn't scare me; it was just a part of our everyday life.

Watching Rachael grow was wonderful. She seemed more delicate than my son did and I felt that she needed more protection because of her medical issues. She was a very happy baby and she smiled a lot. You couldn't tell that she had any medical problems just by looking at her. I was reminded of this every time we went to a cleft palate clinic or other appointments. I saw children in wheelchairs that had tubes attached to them. I also saw children with very noticeable physical deformities. We were very lucky because Rachael looked like a normal blonde-headed little girl with big blue eyes. Every time we had one of these visits I would go home feeling extremely grateful. Most of those parents' lives were consumed by their children's medical issues. I didn't see how they did it day after day. I never stopped to think that others felt the same about my life.

Rachael didn't have any babysitters in her early childhood. None of our close friends were willing to watch her. They were afraid that something would happen while we were gone. They thought she might choke or have some type of seizure. That made going places difficult at times. The situation also made life a bit stressful. It wasn't always easy but that's the way things had to be done. I remember trying to shop for groceries with two young children. I am sure that most mothers can identify with this. Nevertheless, there were times when Rachael would choke and I would have to hold her upside down in the store to clear out her airway. The people around us would stop and stare but I just went about my business. To outsiders, I'm sure that it looked strange but to me it was just part of our normal routine.

Rachael always had doctor's appointments. It seemed as if we had a specialist for just about every part of her body. We even had to go to cleft palate and neurology clinics. It seemed that every month we had more and more appointments. Each time we went, I came back knowing that we were very fortunate. I would see children in wheelchairs and children with tracheas and tubes running from different parts of their bodies, and I knew that Rachael was lucky. People may have felt sympathy for Rachael's situation, but looking at what the other parents were facing made me grateful for her circumstances. I'm not sure I could have gone through what other families were facing on a regular basis. Yes, Rachael had many issues, but when you sum it all up, she was extremely fortunate that her condition wasn't worse. Things in our world didn't look so bad.

Rachael was always healthy as a baby in the general sense. She seemed to be thriving physically. Luckily, for me, she was a happy baby. She was always smiling. At this stage in her life, she seemed to be "normal" like other children. This was good for me because I also had a little boy to take care of. There were days when I would forget that Rachael had health issues.

Children with cleft palates are prone to ear infections. Rachael had her second surgery at eight months and we had tubes placed in her ears as a precaution.

The doctor wanted to make sure that Rachael did not mess with the new hardware in her mouth. Because Rachael was so active, we had to put splints on her hands to keep her from sticking her fingers in her mouth. As you may know, eight-month-olds are always putting their fingers in their mouths. It was a never-ending process because she always managed to find a way to get out of the splints. I had a hard time making sure that they were securely in place at bedtime.

After this particular surgery, Rachael refused to take her formula. I had begun to try her on whole milk at six months and she seemed to enjoy it. We slowly had to incorporate the switch from formula to whole milk. Rachael's appetite also grew after the surgery. I believe that since she was able to keep more of her nutrition down she realized how hungry she actually was. This is when we discovered instant oatmeal. She couldn't seem to get enough of it. She loved the fruit flavored kind. I always made sure that she had an ample supply.

Rachael and her brother, Adam, were close. Adam is eighteen months older than Rachael. They acted and behaved just as siblings do. He was older and mistreated her just as any loving brother would. Rachael was non-verbal but they found a way to communicate with each other. He would often interpret for me and let me know what she wanted. He also did things to her that only brothers can do. He picked on her. A few years later, he intentionally ran over her with his bicycle. Just because Rachael had a disability did not mean she wasn't capable of being a normal child. To Adam, Rachael was just his little sister. He never questioned her differences; he just accepted who she was.

It was around the time that Rachael was three or four that we started to see her stubborn streak. If Rachael was not interested in what she was doing, it didn't happen. She found ways to manipulate everyone around her to get what she wanted. We tried so hard to get her to peddle her little bicycle but she just sat there and waited for someone to push her around. Eventually, she decided she didn't even want her training wheels on, so she tried to take them off. When the training wheels came off, Rachael peddled away. I have come to learn over the years that Rachael does everything in her own way and when she is ready. She does not adhere to anyone's schedule but her own.

Her speech therapists taught her a few words of sign language to help her communicate. Her favorite signs were for McDonalds, French fries, and cookies. She would always let us know if she wanted any of those things. In fact, she had to have another surgical procedure on her palate around this time. The same day she had surgery, she was bouncing up and down on the bed signing for French fries. Fries are not on the list of foods that doctors recommend after any major oral surgery. When the doctor came in, Rachael kept trying to let him know she wanted fries. The next day he brought her a small container of fries.

Due to Rachael's condition, her father and I were asked to see a geneticist for testing. It was during this process we found out both of us carried the gene for *Pierre Robin Sequence*. They asked us some very probing questions. The doctor wanted to know if we were related to each other. I was appalled. I thought he was asking that because we were from Tennessee. I was angry and replied, "Just because I am from East Tennessee does not mean I am related to my husband."

"Yes, I wear shoes," and, "no, I didn't know Elvis." I felt insulted. He seemed to have made unnecessary assumptions. The tests revealed that the odds for us having another child with *Pierre Robin Sequence* were one in three. I had always wanted a big family and this didn't fit into that plan. The risks for Rachael were greater. She has a one in two chance of passing on the sequence. To me, that was the greatest blow. Rachael might not ever be able to have her own children.

After the genetics report, I decided that I shouldn't have any more children. I made an appointment with the Air Force doctor to find out about having my tubes tied. I was told that I was too young and would have to wait until I had another child or was a couple of years older. This meant that I would have to be very careful. I didn't want to bring another child into this world knowing the possibilities that I could have another child with a disability. That may sound selfish, but I didn't feel that I should put that burden on a child if I didn't have to. I wanted to be very careful with birth control.

I began to suffer from severe headaches. I didn't know what was causing it, but I was miserable. One afternoon, after having the same headache for three or four days and vomiting constantly, I went to the emergency room. I was diagnosed with migraines. After a follow-up appointment at the base clinic, I was taken off my birth control medication. This meant I would have to be extremely careful.

I was very diligent about my birth control. I waited until I was old enough and made an appointment to have my tubes tied. While I was waiting, I started to have a problem with a tooth. I ended up having a root canal instead of the tubal procedure. Shortly afterwards Charleston, South Carolina, experienced a hurricane. I became part of the post-hurricane baby boom. I actually knew the minute that it happened. The one time that I wasn't careful, I ended up pregnant again. You can imagine how I felt. I wasn't filled with joy but a mixture of hope and apprehension. I was so afraid that I could have another child with a disability. There wasn't anything that I could do but pray that that wouldn't be the case.

Sara was born in the early morning of July 4. She had a head full of dark hair and she was a screamer. I know that some parents count fingers and toes. I asked the doctors to check her palate. She not only had a soft palate but she also had all ten fingers and toes.

My family was complete. I had my tubes tied the day after Sara was born. When we went home, I didn't have to worry any more about becoming pregnant. Now, I could focus on raising my children. This was a calm period in our lives. I tried to make it a happy childhood filled with the things that little kids like to do.

We went swimming, to the movies, and to the park. Rachael was adjusting to being a big sister. She always wanted to help take care of the baby, but she was jealous from time to time. Once she tried to push me away from Sara because she wanted the attention. I had to pop her on the behind and tell her "no" because this is what I would do to Adam. At this point, the children had typical sibling relationships.

Rachael enjoyed playing with the other kids in the neighborhood. To the other children, she was just a little sister tagging along with her big brother. They all seemed to accept her and played with her. The parents always seemed to have questions. They wanted to know why she didn't talk, why she drooled, and what I was doing about it. Maybe they were just curious, but it still hurt when these things were brought up. I liked to pretend that Rachael was just an ordinary little girl with no issues.

We continued with our many doctor appointments and therapies. I just had one more child to take along with me. It was during a speech therapy session that I discovered that her brother had chicken pox. I spent the next several weeks at home taking care of itchy children. Rachel experienced all of the typical childhood traumas—flu, bumps, bruises, and even stitches.

One time Adam ran over Rachael with his bicycle. Rachael had to have stitches inside of her mouth. She had to be placed on something called a papoose. It was shaped like a surfboard with straps to hold her in place. Her cleft palate made it harder to close up the wound. It was not a pleasant experience for either of us. Later that evening, her stitches became infected and I had to take her back to the hospital.

This would not be the first or the last incident between Adam and Rachael. I couldn't blame him for everything that they got into because Rachael went willingly. If I disciplined him then I had to do the same with her. I wanted the kids to know that I wasn't going to treat them any differently. I wanted Rachael to grow up knowing that just because she had a disability didn't mean that she wasn't accountable for her actions. Sometimes Rachael may not have known any better, but I wanted to set the example of what I expected from her as my child.

I can recall when we had family visiting that they discouraged me from doing this. They would say things such as, "Poor little Rachael, couldn't help it." This upset me because I didn't think of Rachael that way and I didn't want anyone else to either.

Rachael was facing yet another surgery to repair her soft palate. Each time she had a surgery the plastic mold was replaced with a smaller one. The goal was to eventually close it completely and remove the screws. Rachael had had her share of doctors and hospitals and she didn't want to cooperate. She would cry when anyone in a white coat came near her. She didn't take well to the pre-surgery anesthesia cocktails that she was given. She didn't like the out-of-control feeling that it would give her, so she fought it and us. It was hard to watch because I knew she would be going through a surgery and she was suffering before she went. I always cried because it was extremely hard for me to watch them wheel her away.

Rachael had a quick recovery and we went about our daily lives. It always amazed me at how fast she was back on her feet. We were very lucky because it isn't always this way for children and families during the recovery process.

Adam was in kindergarten and Rachael always wanted to go to school with him. It was time to start thinking about pre-school. I didn't know if she would be accepted but I needed to find out. I had no idea on how to go about getting her started. Did I disclose her issues or did I keep quiet? I knew that her speech problems might be an issue, but I had no way of knowing what the school would do about it. I was determined that Rachael was going to school.

EARLY EDUCATION

Rachael began her education in pre-school. She had to be tested prior to entering school. The testing was difficult. It's hard to give a verbal test to someone who doesn't speak. She had a vocabulary of fewer than twenty words. I felt that the tests would be biased against Rachael because she didn't speak. It is scary to think that the results of one set of tests could determine the path that Rachael's education would take.

I was sitting at a small table in a pre-school classroom when I was given the diagnosis that Rachael had mental retardation. I remember that through my tears I just kept saying, "No, you're wrong." I refused to accept the test results. I knew that Rachael had learning problems, but I wasn't prepared for what I was being told. The only thing that kept running through my head was the typical stereotypes of people with mental retardation. In my mind, I kept seeing Rachael's beautiful blue eyes and I knew that she was in there somewhere, even if she couldn't communicate it during the tests. I had to get up and walk out of the room to catch my breath. I was hoping that it was just a bad dream. When I went back, the results remained the same. The diagnosis was real. Like Rachael's medical issues, this was something that I would have to accept.

I had to go home and tell my husband the news. He didn't react badly. He just didn't react at all. It may have been a self-protection mechanism for him, but I didn't get the response that I needed. I wanted him to make it all better or at least say that it would be okay. I wanted him to be the hero and make it all go away. I didn't realize it then but this would eventually be part of the great divide that came between us as parents and spouses.

I had to go through the stages of grief before I could accept Rachael's diagnosis. I asked the entire gambit of Why questions: *Why Rachael? Why us? What will I do? How was this my fault?* I felt helpless. *What would Rachael's life be like?* I knew that I needed to help Rachael but I didn't know how. I couldn't answer any of those questions by myself.

I decided to go back to the people who gave us the diagnosis and ask for help. I have never been good at asking for help but at this point I had no choice. It was the only way I could help Rachael. It was a humbling experience and I had to accept that my daughter was different. She wasn't going to have the life that I dreamed for her. Now instead of looking forward to the future, I was suddenly afraid of it.

We were very lucky because Rachael's pre-school teacher was a very caring person. She was willing to share what she knew with me. This helped me to be a better parent to Rachael. Rachael went to both pre-school and speech therapy. She was still non-verbal but she benefited from the socialization of the classroom. She had friends she enjoyed playing with. It gave her something to look forward to every day.

Before Rachael started kindergarten, we learned that we would be moving out of state. My husband was leaving the military and we were moving home to Tennessee. I was excited because I would have support from our families. There were many times when it was exhausting trying to take care of Rachael and my other children without any help from our families. I had high expectations for our return. On our visits home, everyone had always been great with Rachael. I don't know if it was because we were there for short periods of time, but I thought everyone would just accept Rachael as she was.

Rachael's pre-school teacher gave me some very valuable information before we moved. She told me where to find resources and how to make contacts. Having all of this information proved to be very valuable after the move. I felt that I had the knowledge to begin in a new state and a new education system. I must say that looking back I can see that I was very naive. It takes years to become knowledgeable on special education laws. I wish I had known everything I know now. It is very important to stay well-informed with information that can affect your child's education.

By the time we moved to Tennessee, I had a six-year-old, an eleven-month-old, and Rachael. She was five years old. By this time, I didn't want to disrupt any progress that Rachael had made, so I set about finding her therapists and trying to get her into school. It was overwhelming trying to establish new doctors. I had to become used to not having military health care. We had always been a military family, and I had never realized what a protected world we lived in. We were still covered by the insurance, but I couldn't just make a call and be seen immediately. This was going to be a major adjustment for us. We were no longer entitled to certain benefits. Everything would get a lot rougher before it got better.

I was wrong about the support of our families. Some of our relatives treated Rachael differently. I don't know if it was because they were afraid or ashamed. It was probably a combination of both. It was very hurtful to me and put a strain on several family relationships. My husband ignored it and told me that I was making a big deal out of nothing. I started to realize that I might be in this by myself, at least on an emotional level.

It was the beginning of summer, but I started to work on getting Rachael established with the school system. It was frustrating because I was meeting resistance. I spent a lot of time being angry but found it didn't help the situation.

I can now say that more patience than anger would have helped everything move along faster. Unfortunately, it would take a few more years before I had the ability to apply that principle to myself. I did manage to get the attention of the school system because I was very persistent. There were quite a few obstacles to overcome. The school system wanted to send Rachael to a school across town. I wanted her at the same school as her brother. They didn't seem to want to budge on their decision but neither did I. Eventually, we were able to compromise on that issue and Rachael started the school alongside her big brother.

I went to meet the teachers the first day of school and apparently my reputation arrived before I did. The teacher said that I didn't seem half as scary as the way I had been described. This just goes to show that school officials do take notice of how you present yourself to them. Rachael went on to have a successful experience in an LRE (Least Restrictive Environment) classroom. It turned out that the school was a friendly place. The teachers were very helpful with Rachael. She had a very good kindergarten experience.

During the next summer, we moved to a different school district. This wasn't my idea but my husband felt it was the best choice for the family. This meant that we would have to start over from square one. Rachael was at a point where the differences between her and other children her age were beginning to become more apparent. I began to notice that people would talk to her as if she couldn't comprehend anything that was said. This included family. It made me angry because everyone just made assumptions instead of trying to understand her situation.

I never treated Rachael differently than I did my other children. Okay, that's not entirely true. However, I did my best to raise all of the children with the same beliefs and expectations. If Rachael misbehaved, she received the same punishment as her brother or sister. Even though Rachael had a disability, I wanted to make sure that she could function in a "normal" world. I wanted her to fit into society.

Our new home was in a rural community. It was a different way of life for everyone. The house was old and run down. One room didn't have any siding; it was covered with tar paper. It was not the kind of life that we were used to. It was a new adventure for the kids but it was hard for me. I didn't want to be there but that is where my family was, so I tried to make the best of the situation for the children.

Rachael started first grade at her new school. She had a wonderful teacher and made friends very easily. By this time, I was beginning to learn more about Rachael's educational rights and the current disability laws at the time. I went to workshops and read articles. This taught me how to begin successfully advocating for Rachael's needs. During this time I began having issues with the school. I had learned what guidelines the government built into the educational system to protect children with disabilities. I began to hold the school accountable to timelines and laws that protected Rachael's educational rights. I discovered that knowledge can be a very powerful tool.

I will admit to making waves at the school. When I had an issue with Rachael's educational plan, I took action. I wrote letters, requested meetings, and generally made a nuisance of myself. At one point, I wrote an editorial to the local newspaper. I talked to reporters and to other parents. I could have done some things differently, but I did what I thought was necessary to afford Rachael access to the educational programs she needed. I wasn't just doing it for her. I wanted other families to realize that they had rights too. I earned a bit of a reputation within the school system.

As Rachael progressed in elementary school, her educational program improved. I didn't have to fight as hard. She was very lucky. She had some of the most caring and knowledgeable teachers around. I would never have thought that those types of teachers could have been found in such a rural school system. They worked hard to give Rachael the help she needed. Rachael began to speak a bit more and she found a best friend. It was wonderful to see her fitting in with the other children. It allowed me to forget about Rachael's issues and just concentrate on her being a little kid.

I previously mentioned that I always tried to treat Rachael just as I did my other children. I always tried to encourage all of my children to try new things. When Rachael was in the third grade, she wanted to try out for cheerleader. Now understand, she had a very limited vocabulary and did not speak in front of large crowds. I had mixed feelings. I wanted to say no but I couldn't. I would have been discriminating against my own daughter. This was one of the hardest things I had ever done. It was the first time I allowed Rachael to stand on her own two feet. It was out of my control and I didn't like the way it made me feel.

Rachael tried out for cheerleader. She didn't say a word during the tryouts, but neither did her partner. I cried. I thought she was very brave. My husband thought it was cruel that I let her try out. He thought I should have told her no. He thought I was trying to exploit her. I wasn't. I just wanted her to have the same chances as everyone else.

Rachael did not make the cheerleading team. She also didn't seem too upset by it. I think she just wanted to be part of the activities. Her special education teacher and her speech therapist were proud of her efforts. They got together and had a cheerleading outfit made for her and purchased her some pompoms. She was so proud. She wore her outfit to school with her head held high. It gave her more confidence. She loved the attention. People told her how cute she looked. Something that could have been negative turned into something positive for Rachael. It also had a positive effect on others.

Rachael's experience in elementary school was very good. She bonded with her classmates and they became very protective of her. She made fiends easily and the communication gap did not seem to matter. There were problems along the way, but we faced them one at a time. I would never have thought a rural school could give Rachael the quality of education she received. It just goes to prove that you can't make assumptions about people or school systems until you get to know them.

As is true of many families, our home life was not perfect. We never had a lot of money and we didn't have many extras, but Rachael and the other children seemed to have a happy childhood. Rachael participated in Girl Scouts and church activities. She seemed to be thriving. I couldn't ask for much more than that.

Over the course of elementary school, Rachael had to have several medical procedures. She had the final surgery to close her soft palate and surgery to repair a lazy eye. I looked forward to a time when there would be fewer surgeries and procedures. I don't think it matters how many times you watch a child go through surgery, it never gets any easier. As a parent, you have no control over what happens after they go through the doors of the operating room.

Because of the problems caused by the palate, Rachael had to have multiple dental procedures. She developed a high tolerance for pain. She never really complained and was a true champion. It was very tough for me emotionally to watch Rachael go through all of this. *Pierre Robin Sequence* is a genetic condition and both parents carry the gene sequence. I have always felt responsible for Rachael's condition. Logically, I know it's not my fault but sometimes even after all of this time I still blame myself. Maybe that is one of the many reasons I always fought so hard to keep her life as normal as possible. Whatever the reason, I will do what is necessary to help her achieve a happy and fulfilling life.

***

When Rachael was around ten, she began to realize that she was different from other children. She couldn't always communicate what she felt. This would result in frustration and usually a meltdown. I cannot imagine what that was like for her. It was also hard on her brother and sister. Sometimes no one could figure out what she was trying to tell us. At times, it was heartbreaking and at others, it just left me angry because I couldn't communicate with my own daughter.

Communication breakdowns caused many problems in our home. It wasn't just between Rachael and us but also between me and their father. It was as if he just shut it out of his mind and refused to talk about what was happening. I felt things could have been much better if we had worked together. Instead, I felt as if I were on my own. This happens quite a bit within families of disabled children.

I wanted to find a way to help Rachael communicate more effectively and ease the household tension. I began to ask around for ways to assist her. I turned to teachers and therapists for more help. I looked at devices that would help her communicate with others. I found an organization that would help families like ours. We began to explore communication devices to see whether they could help Rachael communicate with others. She was not very keen on the idea. She thought of them as toys. I decided on one. She would use it at school but not at home. I eventually gave up on the idea. Rachael has always been stubborn when she didn't want to do something. The issue with the communication device was no different. I had to come up with another way to help her communicate.

Rachael loved to write. Therefore, I decided to try teaching her to spell. She had trouble writing a complete sentence, but she did notice individual words. Luckily, she has a good memory. Once she learns a word, it usually stays in her memory. Spelling is a tool that she still uses in her everyday life. When all else fails, Rachael can use spelling to help her communicate.

Rachael didn't let the barriers stop her from being a very social person. She had a few friends who came to our house and she would visit them. It was very good for her. Despite her differences, Rachael found a way to fit in with the kids around her.

***

Two years later, it was time to start thinking about middle school. I was afraid because I didn't know how Rachael would handle the transition. Middle school is much different from elementary school. The structure of classes is different. Rachael would be with children she didn't know. I was worried about how they would treat her. I didn't see how she would be able to navigate going from class to class on her own. The school system didn't offer a program that I felt comfortable with. I spent a lot of time worrying about middle school. I found it would take some creative strategy to get what Rachael needed.

Rachael's teacher worked with me to come up with a plan. We decided that we wanted to skip middle school. Rachael could spend one extra year in the elementary school, and the next year she would spend half of the week at the elementary school and the other half at the high school. This would help her gradually adjust to the changes. Rachael was not a big fan of change. I tried to begin preparing her as far ahead as I could. The hardest part of the plan would be to get the school administration to agree to the plan. I scheduled an IEP meeting.

To make changes in an IEP (Individual Education Plan), a meeting must be held between the parents and the school system. What I was asking for was not the normal policy or procedure. The school tried to argue that if they allowed this for Rachael, they would have to do it for others. What I had to get across was that this wasn't about anyone else. This was about Rachael's education plan. I couldn't worry about what others might need or want at that point. This was about getting what was best for my child. The meeting lasted well over three hours. It was not an easy battle but eventually we were able to come to an agreed arrangement. In my opinion, this was the wisest choice.

Puberty also came calling around this time. This was extremely hard for Rachael. I don't think she was able to comprehend what was happening to her body at this stage of her life. I talked to her about it but she had a hard time understanding the changes she was going through. She had horrible mood swings and that interfered with her communication. This left her more frustrated than normal.

When she started her menstrual cycle for the first time, it was awful. She had trouble understanding how to take care of her hygiene needs. There were many times when she couldn't keep a pad in the correct place and this led to accidents. She was always upset when this happened. She didn't want help from me either. She insisted that she could handle everything by herself, but she was obviously having difficulty doing so. I began to leave extra changes of clothing at school. I figured that this would be less embarrassing for her. This is not an easy time for many young girls, and Rachael's issues further complicated the situation.

When spring rolled around it was time for softball and baseball season. Adam and Sara both played. Rachael had never shown any interest in playing until this time. I think Rachael just wanted to be part of a team. Honestly, I didn't think this would be a good idea. She didn't have a lot of coordination and she was afraid of the ball. I also didn't know how the other girls would react to Rachael. Girls at that age can be cruel. I didn't want them to make fun of her. Rachael hadn't grown up with these girls, so there weren't any developed friendships within the group. It was a scary prospect; however, I also didn't want to deny her the chance to try. She might decide that she didn't like it. I finally gave in and signed her up to play.

The coach and his wife were very nice. I talked to them before the first practice about Rachael's condition. Both of them were teachers and they seemed very receptive to having her on the team. I volunteered to be the team mother so that I could be there to help if needed. It turns out that the girls on the team were wonderful to Rachael. They didn't make fun of her and they actually did their best to encourage her. Rachael wasn't the best ball player. She was your typical extra right field replacement. The coach always let her play and everyone cheered when it was her turn to bat. The most important part of this for Rachael was the fact that she was able to have a uniform and be out there with all of the other girls. She was part of the team. She looked forward to the practices and games. For all intents and purposes, she was just like the other girls.

Rachael usually struck out when she got up to bat. I think she only connected with the ball a few times. Towards the end of the season, something unexpected happened. She was up to bat and she hit the ball. She hit it hard and it flew way out in the outfield. She was shocked and it took a few seconds for her to remember to run. The coach was jumping up and down and the girls on her team were cheering. I was also in shock. As I started cheering there were tears running down my face. I looked around, the coach was crying, and so was the umpire. I tried to pull it together but as I looked around there wasn't a dry eye in the crowd. Rachael had hit a double. It was a moment that I don't think anyone at the game will forget. It was movie ending perfect.

Rachael got a mention at the team banquet for having the most inspiring play during a game. Rachael beamed when she was presented the trophy. The team also gave me a trophy and an autographed ball signed by all of the girls. Today, I still keep them near my desk. Sometimes I will look at them and smile at the wonderful memory it brings back. The moral to this story is that you will never know what is possible unless you try. I have learned this lesson from Rachael many times over the years.

HIGH SCHOOL

High school can be a trying time in any child's life. I think it was much harder for me than it was for Rachael. Many things in our life changed. Children and adults with disabilities don't always deal well with change. Rachael was no exception. I tried to keep everything as normal as possible, but these were changing times for us as a family.

Rachael started high school at 13. She was in a CDC class. This is a self-contained classroom. She spent the majority of her time in the same class. All of the children with severe disabilities were in the same area. She was in a room with children who had physical disabilities, mental disabilities, and mental health issues. I didn't always feel that she was safe, but I had to work and Rachael needed to go to school.

The CDC area had a classroom, a kitchen, and a life-skills area. The children in this classroom setting focused more on life skills than academic work. It seemed as if some were just there to be babysat. This was not what I wanted for Rachael but this is what was available. She enjoyed having friends.

I was working and trying to go to school when Rachael started high school. Rachael's father worked for his father in a family business. He didn't make very much money or have any health insurance. Therefore, I always had to make sure I worked somewhere that provided insurance. It was tough because I couldn't be as involved in Rachael's education as I would have liked. I wish I could have done things differently. At the time, I did not feel as if I had any other options.

Rachael began to develop a special friendship with one of the girls in her class. She had finally found a best friend who was more like her. She had one in elementary school but as they got older, they drifted apart because intellectually they were on different levels. It wasn't anyone's fault. That's just the way life is. It was good to see her have a friend to confide in. They both had speech issues but they found a way to communicate and understand each other. They spent lots of time on the phone laughing and going on as teenage girls often do. It touched my heart to see Rachael talking on the phone and doing things that other girls her age were doing.

Rachael and her friend, Lily, spent a lot of time together. Rachael spent some weekends with Lily and her family. Lily didn't want to stay with us because of her medical issues. That was okay with Rachael. She liked having someone to go places with. One fall, Lilly's mother and I took the girls to see NSYNC in concert. Rachael and Lily screamed and carried on just like the thousands of other girls at the concert.

Rachael also began to notice boys and they noticed her too. This scared me. She was obsessed about having a boyfriend. In her mind, that is what people did in high school. What scared me was the fact that she was so naive and trusting. I didn't want her to be put into a compromising situation just because she wanted a boy to like her. I didn't want her to be taken advantage of or even possibly raped. I was terrified because I knew that I couldn't be there to protect her at all times. I began to think about having her put on some type of birth control.

Rachael began to have more frequent behavioral issues at this time. I don't know if it was because she was frustrated or because she saw other children in the classroom act out. She would have outbursts of unexpected anger. It began to cause issues with her siblings. She would take her anger out on them and then we would go through a cycle of behaviors. She would get angry and scream. She called them names and said hurtful things. Then she would try to hit them and try to lock herself in her room. The final stage was crying. It would take hours for the cycle to complete and there didn't seem to be any shortcuts to get through it. Rachael had to go through each stage. The pattern never changed and it never became shorter or just ended.

I had an opportunity to apply for a much better job with better benefits. Therefore, this seemed like a good choice. The main problem would be my schedule. I would mainly be working the second shift. This would give me a bit more time to work on Rachael's educational issues but I would be away at night. I would have to encourage my husband to help more. He didn't like it, but I tried to make sure I had dinner cooked and had completed any other chores that might need to be finished. Adam and Sara had to take on more responsibility for Rachael. Even though she was younger than Rachael, Sara had to act as the big sister. She helped Rachael in the evenings because I wasn't there. I always felt guilty because in some ways, Sara didn't have a big sister. She had to be the big sister. I regret that I had to put that much responsibility on her at such a young age, but Sara is a much stronger and understanding individual because of it.

Rachael did very well at taking care of her personal needs. She could bathe herself, brush her teeth, comb her hair, and get dressed. She had a few problems but all things considered she did a decent job. Rachael was still having problems with her menstrual cycles. I began to talk with the pediatrician to see if there was anything that could be done to help her. I tried to teach

Rachael to be as independent as possible. I wanted her to be able to care for her personal needs. There would be times when she would have to do things on her own.

It was around this time that my marriage began to unravel. My husband and I wanted different things out of life and we were both very unhappy. I had actually been unhappy for some time but felt that I needed to try to make things work, if for no other reason than the children. There was conflict between us because of the way my husband's family treated Rachael. It always seemed that they talked down to her and acted as if she didn't understand anything. This took a toll on our family life because I wanted my husband to stand up for Rachael and demand that she be treated like their other grandkids. He was her father and I just felt that this would come naturally to him. It didn't. He always denied that there were any problems. He insisted that I was making things up or just imagining it.

We talked about getting a divorce. He always convinced me that there would be no way that I would ever get custody of my children. That is the reason I stayed for so many years. I believed him. That is one of my greatest regrets. I was afraid that I couldn't stand on my own and support the children. Now I know differently. If I've learned anything it's that I am much stronger than I ever thought. I wish I had that kind of confidence in myself back then.

Rachael had a lot of anger during this time. She saw that my husband and I were always arguing. I think this affected Rachael and her moods. I know I should have never let the kids see us argue but it seemed as if we were always fighting. By this time, we didn't talk, we just fought. He never seemed to be there to offer support. His needs and those of his parents came before our family. It was getting harder and harder for me to live with him. Rachael seemed to take a lot of her anger out on her father. I don't think he knew how to handle her behaviors and this caused more issues. I know that he loved her in his own way, but I don't think he understood her.

He was an avid hunter and spent a lot of time away hunting. I was left to deal with most things on my own. This caused even more problems between us. Maybe hunting was his way of escaping from the reality of Rachael's situation. I began to think it would be just as easy to handle things alone because I already felt as if I were alone.

I almost had the courage to take the kids and go when Adam was diagnosed with scoliosis. He was scheduled to have surgery as soon as school was out. This set aside any thoughts I might have had about leaving. His recovery time would be long and we would have to work together as a family to get through it. Both Rachael and Sara were very helpful during this time. I had to concentrate on working and taking care of the children.

Our lives went on and Rachael continued to go to the CDC classroom. I was still going to workshops to learn more about Rachael's rights. Some of the workshops started talking about planning. I wasn't ready to think about that aspect because I assumed that Rachael would be with me long after my other children had left. I began to think it would be great if I could teach workshops like that. I wanted to help others and it would be great to be paid to do it.

Sex is a topic people don't like to discuss, especially if it concerns people with disabilities. I had to face this topic much sooner than I had planned. I had already started talking to the pediatrician about the different options for Rachael. I was always honest with the children about sex, but Rachael did not seem interested or maybe she just didn't understand. She knew about good and bad touches. I don't think she understood the concept of sex.

Adam brought the subject to the forefront. It was just after his recovery from surgery that he told me that his girlfriend was pregnant. I was shocked. I was not ready to hear this from one of my children. This opened my eyes. I had to accept that Rachael could get pregnant. That would have been tragic due to the challenges she already faced and the ones she had yet to face. Adding a child to her struggles would not be a good idea. I also didn't want her to be taken advantage of or to experience that type of trauma.

How could I guard her from sexual predators? I knew that I couldn't always be with her, so I needed to find a way to protect her. I decided to ask the pediatrician for a referral. I needed to find a doctor who worked with girls who had special needs. I thought she should be sterilized. I am ashamed of those thoughts but it seemed to be the best way to keep her safe. Sterilization would protect her from an unwanted pregnancy but not from sexual predators. I felt an urgent need to have this matter addressed. I met with the ob/gyn and he was wonderful. He was very gentle and had a very respectful way of talking to Rachael. He also helped me to have a better understanding of what would be best for Rachael. We decided on Depo-Provera shots. We didn't have to do it every month and it would also stop her periods. The shot was an answer to two problems at once. I didn't have to worry about Rachael getting pregnant or having to deal with her menstrual cycles.

It was a tumultuous time for us as a family. I had to deal with day-to-day life while trying to get ready to be a grandmother. There seemed to be constant strife in the house. We found out that Adam's new family would be joining us in our tiny house. I just didn't see how this would work, especially with all of the fighting going on between my husband and me. I suffered from migraines and they were becoming more frequent due to all of the stress. I needed to make a change that would be best for all of us. I finally realized that I would have to change because my husband wasn't going to.

I decided to take the girls and move out. I tried to talk to them and prepare them as well as possible. I didn't want Rachael to have any difficulties with the changes. My husband and his family didn't think I would actually go through with it. I found a place in the next town and started to prepare the girls for the move. He went away on a long hunting trip and we moved out. I talked to Adam and gave him a choice. He chose to stay where he was because that's where he would begin to raise his own family. It was extremely hard for me to do but I hoped that the few months with his father could help both of them. Rachael took the change well. She flourished without all of the fighting and conflict. I had made the right decision. All the children seemed to accept the changes. Our lives were much more peaceful. My headaches became fewer and Rachael's behaviors improved.

    I started a different job within my department and it gave me a better schedule. I was able to be at home in the evenings for the girls. It was hard to make ends meet but we were happy. We lived there for about six months. I began to have a hard time financially, so I convinced my mother that it would be good for us to move in with her. I was trying to make sure I could give the girls what they needed. It was summer and I didn't have to worry about interrupting the girl's school schedule. I was going to enroll Rachael in a different school system with better opportunities for her. I wanted her to have a chance at a productive life. The county my mother lived in offered more services than where we were.

    The move did not work for any of us. I shared a room with the girls and we were intruding in my mother's space. It's not easy to go back home once you're grown and have a family of your own. My brother decided to move himself and his girlfriend into the house with the rest of us. It became just too much to handle. There was too much drama in the house. Rachael was starting to have some behaviors and I knew I needed to do something. I didn't have many options so I chose the path of least resistance. I moved us back in with my husband. I thought we would try to make it work again. I felt bad about returning but I thought this might be easier for the girls. I didn't feel as if I had any options. So, for a while there were seven of us in a house that was built to hold no more than four people. Rachael and Sara adjusted and life went on. Adam and his family moved into a small house close to us and it gave us more space. Life went on.

Rachael had many dental problems. Her palate and lower jaw caused tremendous problems for her. It seems as if we were always having them worked on. I worked very hard to keep her teeth clean but she fought me. She had braces. The orthodontist was always criticizing me for not taking better care of her oral hygiene. I did the very best I could. I even sent her a toothbrush and toothpaste to school. I had it written into her education plan. The teeth brushing at school did not go well. During this time, Rachael began having more behaviors. I was at my wits' end. I wasn't getting any support from my husband and I was once again very frustrated.

The holidays were approaching and it was stressful. My husband and I were back to fighting and my headaches had returned. We didn't have very much money for Christmas and there was a lot of tension in the house. Rachael began to act out and she directed it towards her father. He wanted to have her put on medication. I disagreed. I wanted to take her to therapy but he was against it. He didn't think that anyone could communicate with her or that she would understand. This caused a lot of tension between us.

We made it through the holidays and I began to think about moving out again. Rachael was seventeen and I needed to concentrate on her future after high school. I didn't want to see her sitting on the couch watching television day after day with nothing to do. There weren't many options in the rural area where we lived, so I needed to come up with a plan for her future.

In February, I had had enough and moved out for the final time. The girls and I moved to a larger city. I did a lot of driving everyday so that they could finish out the school year. Sometimes during the week I even let the girls stay overnight with their father. Rachael seemed to be happy and I tried to help her decide what she was going to do the next year. By law, a child with disabilities can stay in school until the age of twenty-two. I talked to Rachael about this but she said "no." She knew that in high school you were a freshman, then a sophomore, junior and by the fourth year, you became a senior. She had been at the high school for four years and she was ready to graduate to better things. I tried to talk her into staying or getting some type of training but she wasn't interested. Rachael was interested in working and earning a paycheck.

We started going to church just before the move. The church and the congregation became a rock for us. Rachael was accepted for who she was and we all experienced a sense of belonging. Our church family gave us the moral and spiritual support we needed. Rachael enjoyed going to church and making new friends. We started doing some volunteer work as a family through the church. One of the projects was to help feed the homeless. I think those people appreciated Rachael because they could tell that she did it with love and did not have any preconceived notions about them. Rachael was able to give back to others.

During the last semester of high school, Rachael worked in the CDC pre-school as a teacher's helper. She made money and she liked it. Around this time we discovered that Rachael had a passion for shopping. Rachael desperately wanted a steady paycheck. She was tired of school. She was ready for change, which seems ironic. Academically she wasn't making any progress so I thought it might be the best thing for her. In hindsight, I wish I had been able to push harder for her to get more help with her academics during her school years. I still look back and think I failed her in some ways. Knowing everything that I do now, I would have pushed harder and been more involved.

It was almost time for the prom. Rachael hadn't been asked but she and her best friend wanted to go. Rachael's father was against her going. He didn't think it was appropriate.

He tried to talk me out of letting her go but I wasn't going to let her miss out because of him. Rachael was excited and had a dress picked out. She went with her best friend and her friend's father escorted them to the prom. Both girls had a wonderful time. They enjoyed getting dressed up and having flowers. I think Rachael will always remember that evening. I am so glad that she was able to experience it. I still don't understand why her father didn't want her to have that experience.

Rachael's graduation date was quickly approaching. I had so many mixed emotions. I didn't know what Rachael would do after school. I was scared and was afraid of crossing that bridge. I knew that we had reached that time. I always assumed that Rachael would want to live with me. I didn't think much about her having plans of her own.

I tearfully made it through graduation. We had a big party for Rachael with family at our house. I had a picture of her put on the cake. She had a great time. It was hard for me to accept that my little girl was finished with high school. Rachael was ready for her next adventure.

***

Rachael was ready but the adventures weren't ready for her. I had to begin the process of getting her registered for services. I encountered problems because Rachael wasn't yet eighteen. We filled out paperwork and signed up for a disability conference as a family. We were able to get a stipend to attend the conference. The information from this conference would prove valuable in the future.

The more involved we became in trying to get the programs started, the harder it was for me to take off from work. My job demanded that I always be there. This put a lot of pressure on me also because I had to leave Rachael at home alone. I would go check on her at lunch but it was still hard to do. She called me one day to tell me that the mail was on fire. I was so scared. I pictured her burning to death in the house. I left immediately. I ran a few red lights on my way to the house. I rushed home expecting to find fire trucks outside of the house. When I arrived, everything looked normal from the outside. I went in to a smoky house but there was no fire. The fire was out because she put the mail in the sink and turned on the water. She had neglected to tell me that before I rushed home. Rachael always put the mail on the stove and it seemed okay because she never cooked on the stove. This particular day she had decided that she wanted to have oatmeal. She always used the microwave to make her oatmeal. I don't know why she decided to use the stove. That incident made me realize that Rachael needed to be doing something other than sitting at home alone. She also needed some type of supervision.

 I begin trying harder to get Rachael into a good program. I was having trouble concentrating at work. It didn't help that Rachael's paternal grandmother worked in my department. There had always been tension between the two of us but it was now much worse, especially where Rachael was concerned. I would hear her talking to someone about Rachael. She didn't refer to her as her granddaughter but as "Donna's daughter." She didn't even acknowledge that her son was Rachael's father. Things like this were very painful for me to hear. I couldn't believe that someone who was supposed to be family could make such comments about Rachael. I was miserable and needed to make a change.

 I wasn't much help to Rachael at this time. I decided to walk away from my job. This also included any benefits that came along with it. Everyone thought I was crazy. I didn't have any money to fall back on but I knew it would be the best decision for our family. I was still married and hadn't filed for divorce yet. I can't explain why I waited for so long. I wanted to make sure I was doing the right thing, and part of me still held out hope that my husband would step up and do the right thing.

I wasn't going to return just because it would have been easier on me financially. I had already tried that. I never seemed to have enough money but I knew that I had to walk away from my job. I had to take care of myself before I could begin to help Rachael. I could not do either of those while I was working that job. I was making progress towards finding Rachael a program that would help her find a job. This was the main goal that I had to focus on. It wasn't easy but we made it through. The tough times helped to bring the girls and me closer to one another.

Months passed and Rachael was beginning to become a bit frustrated because she was tired of being at home. She told me that she wanted to move and to be with her friends. "We weren't fun." I think she resented the fact that Sara was involved in so many school activities and she wasn't. Sara also had many friends. Rachael began to take some of her frustrations out on her sister. Sometimes Sara would call me from the bathroom. She was hiding because Rachael had tried to attack her. Rachael had returned to the pattern of behaviors that she had experienced before. We seemed to be constantly going through her emotional cycles. It was very tough and I wasn't sure about what I should do. I could only hope and pray that once Rachael had a job she would be happier.

It was a very trying time. Luckily, we had support from our church and friends. This helped to keep me going. I began cleaning the church to try to help make ends meet. I was also picking up cooking jobs. I never got more than a few hundred dollars for child support the entire time that my husband and I were separated. My vehicle was repossessed. It was an extremely tough time personally and financially but I knew that I was doing the right thing.

I learned a lot about myself during this time. I knew that I was determined to do whatever it took to get Rachael the services she needed.

TRANSITION

FROM CHILDHOOD TO ADULTHOOD

Transition is the process of change. This chapter deals with how Rachael transitioned from being a child with disabilities to being an adult with disabilities. The moment she turned eighteen, she no longer qualified for many of the services she had received as a child.

Rachael is a very capable individual. If you were to read about her in a report, you might not be able to make the connection between the person on the paper and the real Rachael. According to testing and governmental reports, Rachael qualifies to live in a nursing home. Just because a document makes a statement doesn't necessarily mean that the situation is as black and white as the words on the page. As Rachael's mother, I know that she is much more capable than what any piece of paper might say. Unfortunately, you need those types of reports to acquire needed services. It can be a double-edged sword.

Rachael needed to register for services. I began the process as soon as she graduated from high school. I had to take Rachael to different offices and fill out a tremendous amount of paperwork.

Every aspect of services for individuals with disabilities is handled by a different agency. It was hard for Rachael to understand that it takes time for services to begin. Patience is not one of Rachael's best character traits. I must admit she inherited the trait from me. Rachael was willing to go wherever we needed if I thought it would help and because it got her out of the house for a while. I wanted to gather as much information as possible. There are many resources, but you may have to hunt for them. Asking questions is important. There are no wrong questions, just the ones you don't ask. So I asked lots of questions. I didn't always get the answers I wanted, but I was often pointed in the right direction.

I have to admit that I never spent a lot of time thinking about what Rachael wanted to do with her life. I thought that Rachael and I would always be together. When Rachael began to receive services, part of those programs included self-determination classes. Rachael must have been listening because she became very determined. She began to let me know that she had opinions and rights. She even had the nerve to tell me that I worked for her. She actually fired me a few times. It took me by surprise because she had never expressed her opinions about her rights or her future. Because Rachael has a disability, I had never thought to ask her what she wanted to do with her life. I'm not proud of this but it is fact. Rachael began talking about having a job, a car, and a bank account. She was adamant that you needed these three things when you turned eighteen. She told me that her cousin, who was the same age, had all of this and she wanted to know when it was her turn. I couldn't come up with an argument against what she wanted. It made me stop and think about the way I had been looking at things. I wasn't ready to let Rachael live her life. This was an eye-opening revelation for me because I had always considered myself open to Rachael having the same opportunities as the other children. It didn't happen overnight but I did come to terms with it. The hard part would be to start making her dreams a reality.

Rachael and I had to choose a service provider. Their focus was trying to find her a job. I had to promise her that when she found a job, I would get her a bank account. She wanted the bank account so that she could have a bankcard. The car was a different story. Rachael doesn't drive. She probably never will. How could I explain this to her? I have always encouraged her to try new things, so how could I tell her that she couldn't drive? In the end, I didn't have to. One of the support agencies that Rachael had registered with offered a driving course geared for individuals with different learning abilities. The course would teach the driving manual, provide opportunities to practice on a simulator, and eventually take the student to the department of motor vehicles to take the test. I didn't think Rachael could pass the class but she wanted to try. Reluctantly, I agreed. Remember, this was about what she wanted and not what I wanted. I was trying to practice what I had been preaching all of these years. It just seemed much easier when she was younger because I never thought about her wanting to have her own life. That's hard for me to admit as a parent, but that's the way it was.

Rachael began to go to the classes. She had a lot of trouble with the bookwork. She just didn't understand the material. We would work on it in the evening, but she just didn't comprehend it. It broke my heart to watch, but I had to allow her to complete this on her own. This is what I would do if it had been one of the other children. Pass or fail, I had to let her do it on her own. One afternoon, she came back crying and just saying, "I can't, no more." Rachael made the decision to quit. I had to let her make the choice because it wasn't mine to make. It was very hard to sit back and watch from the sidelines but I had to for Rachael. She still talks about learning to drive one day. Perhaps in time we will try again.

The service provider finally found a job for Rachael. She was scheduled to start after the Christmas holidays. She would be working as an usher at a local movie theater. She was excited because the job was located at the mall. Finally, Rachael felt as if she had a purpose. She constantly reminded me that if she had a bankcard she could go shopping. As you can imagine, that prospect really thrilled me. I had to remind her that you have to have money in the bank before you can shop. Rachael was very excited because she would be wearing a uniform. All was good in the world of Rachael. When things are good there, they are good in everyone else's universe.

A few questions had to be answered before Rachael started the job. *First, how would she get there?* She didn't drive and I couldn't always be her transportation because I also had a job. I found out that the city bus system offered a shuttle service for individuals with disabilities. She could be picked up at our front door. She would be dropped off at the mall and they also made the return trip. The major problem with the service was that you had to call and arrange the pickups in advance. There was also a positive side to having Rachael use the bus system. If the bus was running late, I could call the dispatch office and find out exactly where they were along the route. That gave me comfort and I felt that she would be safe.

Second, how would she learn where to catch the bus? Rachael's job coach taught her how to navigate the bus system. She practiced riding with Rachael. They rode from the house; they rode back from the mall and learned the route.

The first day Rachael rode the bus alone, the job coach was waiting for her at the mall. She wanted to see if Rachael could ride the bus alone. Rachael didn't have any problem with this but I did. That is why they didn't tell me until after it took place. I am guessing the job coach knew I would have been a basket case.

Third, how would Rachael know when it was time to come back from her break? Rachael couldn't tell time, so a watch wasn't the answer. We decided to use an egg timer. Rachael learned how to set the timer for fifteen and thirty minute intervals. This worked out well, so she kept it in her locker.

Fourth, how would Rachael converse with customers? We applied for assistance from the technology access center. They provided a communication device that she wore on her wrist. It was no bigger than an iPod. (We looked at larger devices but Rachael didn't think they were cool.) The device had the capability of storing up to ten phrases. The phrases were programmed so that she could assist customers with directions.

All of my questions were answered before Rachael started working. Finding out the answers before she started working helped me to feel more secure with Rachael riding the bus to work.

I worried about how Rachael would interact with her coworkers. I had tried to teach her right from wrong, but I wasn't sure how she would do on a public work site. Her job coach worked with her for about a month on the job. She made sure Rachael understood the rules of working with the public. She also helped to show her what was appropriate and what was not when dealing with coworkers. This was a tremendous help, especially since I couldn't be there to do it myself. Gradually, the coach faded out of the picture until she was just calling the manager to find out if Rachael was having any difficulties. Rachael also established friendships with her coworkers. They became very protective of her. She seems to bring that quality out in people. Rachael completed her trial period and was hired as permanent part-time movie theater usher, so I had to give in and set up a bank account.

I mentioned earlier that Rachael's job was located at the mall. She loved to go shopping, so her breaks were spent looking and sometimes shopping. She developed a love for purses and large hoop earrings. The store clerks knew her by name because she visited them on a daily basis. Her math skills weren't very good. Therefore, the bankcard was easier for Rachael to use because she had trouble with counting money. The hardest part was trying to ensure that she didn't overspend. Occasionally she did, and her first and last major shopping spree caused me to take her card away. In this way she was just a typical teen going overboard at the mall.

The shopping spree happened when I was traveling for my job. I was in another state and I received a call from one of her managers asking if I could pick her up. She was so busy shopping that she had missed the bus. I was eight hours away but I still had to make calls and arrange for alternate transportation. She was staying with her father but he didn't want to come and get her, so I ended up getting another family member to pick her up. Her father tried to use this incident to convince me that Rachael shouldn't be riding the bus or working at the mall. It didn't matter how much he complained. Rachael needed to ride the bus to get to work. Her job was located at the mall and I wasn't going to take that away from her. I had to work and since he wasn't willing to help with her transportation, she continued to ride the bus.

I also found out upon my return that Rachael had spent well over two hundred dollars that she didn't have. I took Rachael's card away and made her repay the charges. Rachael's father thought that I had been irresponsible to let her have a bankcard to begin with. He blamed me for everything. I felt that she made a mistake just like most kids do and had to pay the same penalty, but I never thought that it was wrong to have given her the opportunity.

I did learn that I needed to take a few precautions to avoid having this happen again. I went back to having Rachael use cash. Rachael had to divide her paycheck and could only keep the amount that she could afford to spend. Rachael now knows how to stay within her shopping budget. She doesn't go over her limit, but she will spend until she reaches that point.

Rachael made another decision about what she needed. Can you see where this might be going? She decided that she needed a cell phone. I decided that this was probably a good idea so that we could stay as close as a phone call away. I purchased a prepaid phone that she could use when she needed to call me. She was satisfied with this for a while. She told me that everybody else could take pictures with their phones and she couldn't. I promised that we would start looking.

I put it off for as long as possible. In the meantime, Rachael started looking for herself. She changed the stores that she usually shopped at for stores that sold cell phones. One day she conned me into going in the mall instead of just picking her up. She took me directly to Radio Shack. She could have gotten a free phone but it didn't have a camera in it, so we had to continue searching.

She found what she wanted but with the cost of the phone and the deposit, we were looking at around two hundred and thirty dollars. I told Rachael that I couldn't afford that much money, so she would need to save her money until she had enough. Honestly, I thought she would forget about it if she had to wait. She saved until she had enough money and she purchased the phone. It had all kinds of features including the camera. One thing that you should know about Rachael is that she never forgets and is very determined if something is important to her. Rachael always remembers the promises that you make to her. I've learned more lessons from her with that cell phone than I care to admit. Rachael's phone is a big part of her world. I found it very ironic that she didn't speak during her early years and now she was buying a cell phone.

Another important part of transition is independent living skills. Most special education classes teach some of the skills in school and it was no different for Rachael. She still had a long way to go, but that's also true of most typical eighteen-year-olds. I wanted to make Rachael independent so she could take care of her basic needs. She did well with hygiene and taking care of her belongings.

She knew how to clean her room but sometimes her room looked as if a bomb had exploded. In other words, it wasn't much different from any teen's room across the country. I wanted her to be able to handle as many aspects of the household chores as she could.

The first thing I decided to teach her was how to do laundry. I wanted her to be able to take care of her own clothes. I had to figure how I would go about this. I decided to make her some charts that listed how much detergent and fabric softener to use. I showed her how to divide her laundry into separate baskets. I also made the decision just to use cold water. This way I didn't have to worry about her putting clothes in at the wrong temperature; it also saved money.

I found that dry laundry detergent and dryer sheets worked the best. One of the most exciting days for me was when I came home from work and went to the laundry room to see what needed to be washed. To my surprise, it was empty. Rachael had washed and dried everything on her own and had even put the clothes away. She was so proud. I was overjoyed because I have never had to do her laundry since. My little girl was growing up and becoming independent.

Cooking is another skill that is needed to be independent. Having a microwave can make this possible for individuals who don't have great cooking skills. Rachael still doesn't cook on the stove very often but she can use the microwave like there's no tomorrow. I wanted to encourage her to spend time in the kitchen, so I decided that both Rachael and Sara would take one day each week and prepare the evening meal. I didn't care if it was peanut butter and jelly sandwiches or cereal as long as they fixed it and cleaned up after themselves. I enjoyed the freedom of not having to cook every night. Rachael discovered that for less than ten dollars she could buy a pizza and soda. This fed all three of us and she did not have to wash any dishes. Generally, on Rachael's night to cook, we had pizza. It wasn't a bad deal for any of us.

Rachael can do an excellent job of cleaning the kitchen. In the beginning, I had to make a list of everything that was included. This meant not just washing the dishes but wiping counters and the table. Sometimes it was frustrating because she did not always get the dishes clean. I would have to go behind her and rewash them. I would wait until she had gone to sleep so that she never knew. I wanted to encourage her to keep trying because sometimes she would get angry if she tried something new and it did not work. She would just refuse to do it anymore. This was the last thing I wanted. It just took practice, and the more that she did it the easier it became.

A big part of becoming an adult is learning how to keep up with your schedule and appointments. Obviously, Rachael needed assistance in making her appointments, especially if it was over the phone. I did that for her because I didn't want her to become frustrated. I also wanted her to be responsible for her appointments. I thought it would be easy for her because she has such a good memory. Rachael had a calendar that she kept all her information on. She brought home her work schedule and put it on the calendar. She made sure that I called to schedule transportation and then she would count out how many tickets it would cost for the week. (The bus that picked her up took one ticket each way. Each ticket cost two dollars.) Rachael also takes a daily medication. She is able to self-medicate and has always been very vigilant when taking her medicine. She would let me know about when she was down to one or two pills so that I could call for a refill. Details like this have helped her to become more independent. It puts her in more control of her life. I want her to have as much control as she can.

Rachael is very punctual and she expects everyone else to be the same way. If she was waiting on the bus and it ran more than ten minutes late, she would call me and ask me to find out where the bus was. She wanted to make sure she wasn't late for work. She is very concerned about being at work on time. She is always concerned about doing the best job she can. Part of doing a good job is being at work on time. I admire that quality in her.

Rachael has an excellent memory. She remembers birthdays and anniversaries far better than I ever will. If they aren't on my calendar, I might forget, but Rachael does a good job of reminding me. She doesn't do it as much as she used to, but she used to tell us what day of the week someone's birthday would fall on. The way her memory works sometimes is just amazing. That is another reason that if you make her a promise, you had better keep it. Otherwise, she will remind you repeatedly. I believe this helps her with her independence.

Socialization is also part of transition. Rachael is a very social person. She likes to stay busy and she wants to be going somewhere constantly. Since Rachael doesn't drive, this means that I have spent a big part of my time going different places. Rachael likes going to church, visiting relatives, going to football games, and of course shopping. Rachael wanted to do things with friends. Up until this point, she didn't have a lot of friends she could hang out with. She would see her sister going over to stay with friends or having friends coming over and she was jealous. Sara's friends accepted Rachael and were always kind to her. Rachael would try to infiltrate the group and pretend that she was part of the crowd. There were times when this was okay, but other times it caused conflict between sisters. I didn't want Sara to feel that Rachael was being forced upon her and her friends. I needed to figure out a way for Rachael to have some social interaction of her own.

I was working for a non-profit organization that helped families who had children with disabilities. This was a major help for me because I had access to programs that Rachael could participate in. I found out about a program that would allow Rachael to socialize and do fun and interesting things every day. The program would also drop her off at work on the days she was scheduled. The only problem was that the program was aimed at high school seniors. We had a few things in our favor. Rachael was still the right age, I had a few connections to the program, and she had the funding in place for the program.

Funding becomes very important in what programs individuals are allowed to participate in. Sometimes it comes down to finding a way to pay for the programs. Sometimes you have to search out creative avenues to find the money to pay for programs.

Rachael enjoyed the program. She made new friends and was able to participate in so many activities. The program even came with its own drama. It was just like high school. The kids worried about who liked whom and who said something bad about someone else. Rachael loved being right in the midst of it all.

The interaction and drama did cause a few problems along the way. Rachael would get upset if one of her friends was upset. She didn't express this at first. She would just become angry and agitated. This sometimes led to the behavior cycle that she would go through, and it wasn't until we arrived at the tearful stage that we would find out what exactly was the catalyst. Those behavioral cycles would leave the whole family exhausted and frustrated. Rachael always involved anyone who happened to be in the house at the time. Rachael also picked up behaviors from her friends. I had tried to prevent this because I didn't want Rachael to act out this way in public. I didn't want Rachael to draw unwanted attention because she was exhibiting a certain type of behavior. It has been successful but sometimes the whole family must get involved. For example, Rachael wanted to hug and pat everyone. This drew unwanted attention, so I wanted to find a way to stop it. We started patting Rachael consistently, sometimes before she did it to us. She didn't like it and after several months she stopped.

Sometimes when Rachael acts out, we ask her how old she is. Then we ask whether someone that age would do the same thing. If all else fails, we ask her whether it's appropriate. When she's asked whether doing something is appropriate, it seems to trigger something in her brain and she stops. I can't explain why it works, but it does.

Rachael had been working on her independent living skills. I tried to give her as much space as possible. I wanted her to feel as if she had some grownup freedoms. She noticed that her coworkers had apartments and that even her friends in the programs had their own spaces. Rachael wanted her own space. She didn't want to live with me. She wanted to move out as other people her age did. I know that Rachael can't live totally independently. I am also not crazy about her living in a group home. A group home is where a small group of individuals live with staff to assist them with their needs and supervise the household. Usually, anywhere from five to eight people share a home. So, I began to search for a solution that we could all live with. Initially, I didn't have a clue as to what I would do, but I knew it was important to Rachael. The issue wasn't going away.

I decided to move into a larger house that would provide Rachael with her own space. She would have her own apartment. She had three rooms—a bedroom, a bathroom, and a living room and dining room combination. She would need to use the main kitchen but she would also have her own space. She wanted a mini fridge to keep her sodas and snacks. I looked at the cost and decided to buy a used household refrigerator. This way, we could use the extra space if needed. Rachael wanted her own microwave, so she had to save enough money to buy one.

Through friends and relatives, I found a loveseat, a recliner, and a dining room table. Rachael had her own apartment including her own entrance. This apartment met both my requirements and Rachael's. She was able to be more of an adult and I knew she would be safe. Rachael had to keep her apartment clean, but on several occasions she informed me that it was her apartment and she didn't have to clean it unless she wanted to.

I had to reinforce the fact that cleanliness was a condition of keeping the apartment. Young adults are notorious for messy apartments. Rachael also enjoyed her privacy. Sara and I were asked to leave many times. Rachael needed "privacy please." This was Rachael's sanctuary and she enforced this. You could come and watch television, but you had to ask first and if you wore out your welcome, you were asked to leave.

We have always had pets, so Rachael has grown up with them. She has learned to help feed, water, and walk them, but she never had an animal that was her sole responsibility. Rachael began to ask for a cat. Her friends had one in their apartment, so she thought she should also.

Cats are fairly easy to take care of except for changing the litter box. I wanted no part in that. Rachael received a cat for Christmas. I picked it up a few days early because I knew that our very large dog would have to get used to it.

The look on Rachael's face when she saw the kitten was priceless. She looked at him as her baby. She did a good job taking care of him, but sometimes she had to be reminded about the litter box. The main problem was keeping the dog from eating him. We had to keep a vigilant watch and make sure that when we were gone the dog couldn't get to him. Someone was constantly on "save the cat patrol."

It took a good three months for the dog to become used to the fact that the cat wasn't going away. Rachael makes sure the cat has enough food and water. She also lets me know if we need to buy cat food or litter. Sometimes she will purchase it herself. This shows a lot of progress towards her transition into adulthood. She is learning to take responsibility for others.

I don't know whether Rachael will ever be truly independent. If she has a proper support system, she can achieve a certain level of independence. She always reminds me that she's a "big girl" and, "You can't tell me what to do." My goal is to have her be as independent as possible and yet make sure she is safe. I want her to have a fulfilling life and enjoy all it has to offer. I don't want her just sitting on the sidelines as the world goes by. I want to see her out there marching to the beat of her own drum.

Rachael will always be transitioning to each new phase of her life. It is my intent to help prepare the path so she will lead a safe and rewarding life. After all, that's what we want for all our children. I try to plan ahead as much as possible. It's not always easy to anticipate just what the future may hold, so it usually works best to have a few backup plans.

Rachael is now at a phase where she is wrapped up in the relationships she has formed with friends. She has a boyfriend and just like all the other girls her age she wants to date. In her situation it's just not as simple as dating. Her boyfriend lives in a group home. He doesn't have the same freedoms Rachael has. If Rachael wanted to invite him over, she would just ask her parents. But for individuals in a group home, it is a much different situation.

Individuals who live in a group home must go through caseworkers, staff schedules, and a lot of red tape. The protocols are there for the protection of the individual. It does make it almost impossible for them to make any spontaneous plans. I've had to do a lot of explaining so Rachael can understand this. She still asks me almost every day if her boyfriend's staff has called me. Rachael is learning a valuable lesson. She doesn't like the group home procedure, so she is having to learn patience. She seems to enjoy the freedom she has here at home.

RELATIVELY SPEAKING (PART 1)

Families are complicated organisms. If you add in a family member with a disability, it can become even more complicated. People don't always react positively to someone with a disability. It may not be done out of malice, but most families treat individuals with disabilities differently. Rachael's family is not any different from others in this way.

Rachael was just a bit different from other babies. She looked the same on the outside, but she was missing her soft palate. When Rachael ate, part of it always came back out her nose. She always seemed messy. There never was any hint of how much food would make it down into her stomach or how much would make a return appearance. She also drooled a lot. This was due to her small jaw and the fact her tongue was longer than normal. She didn't quite know how to hold it in place.

She was generally healthy and had an even temper. She was a good baby but she had feeding issues. There were many times when I felt as if family members thought I was being a bad mother because she got messy at mealtime. Some of the feelings I had were most likely imagined. I was very young and I did not have a healthy self-esteem. I always felt as if I was being judged because my daughter had a disability.

When she was a toddler, family members didn't treat Rachael any differently than they treated her brother. She didn't talk but in every other aspect she seemed "normal." It was easy for me to pretend at this point that there weren't any issues. I could just stick my head in the sand and tell myself the disability was only in my imagination. As Rachael's baby teeth came in, they were the size of permanent teeth. (They didn't come in until she was a toddler.) They looked even larger because her mouth seemed so tiny. Both sides of the family offered me advice on what I needed to do. The problem with that is that no one knew anything about cleft palates. Perhaps they had good intentions, but the advice seemed condescending. I was treated as if I didn't care that she was having problems with her teeth. I was very much aware of those issues. I needed support not accusations. No one seemed willing to understand. Even now, Rachael's teeth are shaped a bit differently. She has been through numerous oral surgeries and braces. There are probably a few things that can still be done. I would not put her through any more procedures just for cosmetic purposes. That would have to be Rachael's decision.

The older Rachael became the easier it became to see the developmental differences between her and Adam. She spoke very few words and often grunted to let you know what she wanted.

Family members told me I shouldn't encourage the grunting. This was Rachael's way of communicating and is something I did encourage. I wanted her to know I saw she was trying to communicate. In my mind, any form of communication was better than none at all. Rachael was taking speech therapy but wasn't making much progress. Adam seemed to understand her and they were able to communicate with each other. Grunting kept her from being so frustrated when she was trying to let someone know what she wanted. I expected her to eventually get past this phase and start talking.

It was about this time relatives began to react differently to Rachael. I would notice they talked and acted in a different way than when they interacted with Adam. This really made me angry. I tried to voice my concerns but they went unnoticed. It was very hard for me because Rachael's father just pretended it wasn't happening. On top of being angry, I was hurt because my husband didn't give me support when dealing with his family.

Children are children even if they have disabilities or issues. Despite what some may think, children notice when they are being treating differently. It is as if they can sense it. They understand there is a difference and they have no way to express how it makes them feel. I hated thinking Rachael was sensing the different treatment. People can't help the way they feel but they can help the way they react. It is my belief that children notice this type of behavior in adults. That is one reason I have tried so hard to make sure I never did that to her. I wanted Rachael to feel just as loved and wanted as the other children in the family.

I have never felt sorry for Rachael, but I did feel responsible for her condition. During genetic testing, I was told that my husband and I both carried the gene necessary for *Pierre Robin Sequence* to occur. There were always thoughts that ran through my mind for ways I could have prevented Rachael from having to live with a disability. I also thought that if I had married someone else, Rachael would have been completely healthy. It was strange but I never truly blamed Rachael's father. I felt the burden needed to fall on me. I had a few pity-parties for myself and then I would go about my business.

I have found that many parents, especially mothers, have felt this way at some point in time. We tend to blame ourselves for the situation. The facts are that we are not responsible for our child's disability. We shouldn't obsess if it's a genetic condition we passed along, because somehow it was passed along to us. Others may judge us but we can't let that get to us. They have not spent any time walking in our footsteps. It's taken me years to realize this, but it's a piece of advice every parent should have.

I knew I needed to be strong for Rachael. I could not let her or anyone else see how much this affected me. I wanted Rachael to have a normal life. What hurts the most from this time in my life is that I didn't have anyone to confide in or get support from. It's really sad to think that my husband and I didn't communicate or support each other. The lack of support and communication is what drove a wedge between Rachael's father and me. Unfortunately, you see this type of reaction between couples when they have a child with a disability. A child with a disability can either bring a family closer or tear it apart.

I don't think Rachael's father knew how to react to her as she grew older. I know he loved her in his own way, but I am not sure he has ever accepted her for who she was. Maybe he felt some guilt of his own. I don't know because he never talked about his feelings. I always felt that part of him was ashamed of her. I think the situation embarrassed him. I honestly don't know and am assuming. Unfortunately, I may never know for sure.

We both came from families who didn't believe in expressing feelings. I have to say that neither of us had good communication models growing up. It would have benefited us as a couple if we had sought counseling to help us deal with the situation.

Rachael's father never took an active role in her education. I couldn't get him to go to trainings or to meetings. He never participated in IEP meetings. I am not even sure he knows what IEP (Individual Education Plan) stands for. Maybe he felt as if he couldn't handle them. I wish he had wanted to be involved. This caused a lot of hostility between the two of us. He never wanted to talk about it, so I had to let it go.

I feel that it is important for both parents to work together to further a child's education. This is especially true of children with disabilities. It would have been extremely helpful to have someone to discuss matters with and to help me make decisions. We could have been a much stronger family if we had worked together to help Rachael reach her educational goals.

From my experiences, I urge families to talk to one another. Share your feelings; it doesn't help to hold everything inside.

Rachael has two biological siblings who grew up with her. Rachael's brother and sister treated her just like any other sibling. They would be playing with each other one minute and fighting the next. I never felt that either one was ashamed of Rachael. I think that they may have felt burdened because both of the kids had to help take care of her. I am sure there were times when having Rachael for a sister wasn't very easy. They had to be more protective of her and there were many times when someone would make fun of her. They were always there to defend her honor. Both Adam and Sara treated her with respect and love. Maybe it's because they grew up with her and there wasn't any special treatment for Rachael from me. They came to know Rachael as a sibling and not as a sibling with a disability. I believe that as they have grown up they are more receptive to others with disabilities. I admire both of them for having those qualities.

That did not mean the children didn't fight amongst themselves. There were times when they fought like cats and dogs. I have to say Adam was the biggest instigator. He was always trying to talk Rachael into doing things she shouldn't. She trusted her brother and she fell right into his little traps. Usually someone would get hurt and most of the time it was Rachael.

Once when Rachael was about three years old, Adam decided she was dirty, so he took Spray–n-Wash to clean her face. His efforts to clean his sister resulted in several hours in the emergency room while she had her eyes washed out. In Adam's defense, I should point out that he experienced many trips to the hospital for his own mishaps. It just goes to show that kids will be kids. Adam did things to Rachael not because she had a disability but because she was his sister. This automatically made her fair game.

Today Adam is grown and has a daughter of his own. I think his experience of having a sibling with a disability has made him a better parent. He has never talked about his feelings. He is a lot like his father in that respect. In my heart, I feel that if he had a child with a disability, he would be very involved.

Sara is five years younger than Rachael but they had a lot of things in common when they were younger. Sara has always been very caring with Rachael. At times it seemed as if Sara was the older child. She took on many extra responsibilities. Sometimes I still feel guilty about this. I feel as if Sara had to grow up faster than she needed to. I will say that the experiences she had with Rachael have helped to develop her into a leader. I feel that she also has a good deal of empathy for people with disabilities.

I do need to mention that both Adam and Sara have a disability of their own. They have scoliosis. It is not genetic but they have the same type. This is very ironic in itself. Rachael liked to remind them that finally they had an issue that she didn't. I think it was her way of teasing them. I can proudly say that neither Adam nor Sara have let scoliosis get in the way of having fulfilling lives.

Rachael grew up with two sets of grandparents and they reacted very differently to her. My parents were more accepting. I am not saying that because they were my parents. They did their best not to make a difference between the kids. I can say that my father had a special spot in his heart for Rachael. I remember once when my in-laws took the children shopping. They bought Adam a pair of cowboy boots and a hat. Rachael got a doll. My father felt that Rachael had been slighted and he was furious. He gave my mother money to go out and buy Rachael something nice. You have to understand, my father was very stingy when it came to money. It was actually quite shocking to see him open up his wallet and willingly hand out money. During my life, I only saw him cry once and it was when Rachael had surgery. He passed away when Rachael was only six years old, but I know he continues to watch over her. He would be very proud of the person she has become.

My mother had previously been around a family member with a disability. She had a second cousin with mental retardation. I think she has been able to identify with some of the issues Rachael has faced. She has always been supportive of all of the things I have done to help Rachael. She has never made any differences between Rachael and her other grandchildren.

Rachael's other grandparents gave me the feeling they were ashamed of her. I don't think it was a conscious act, but it did affect how they reacted to Rachael. They never spoke to me about it so I may never know how they felt. After the divorce, they only saw Rachael on holidays or maybe once or twice each year at a cookout. I never tried to keep them from her. They have always had the option of staying in contact with Rachael. I used to try to force Rachael into spending time with them if it became available. Now that Rachael is older, she has no trouble seeing that they treat her differently. She used to ask why they didn't call her or try to see her. I think it really hurt her feelings.

This is the first year (during the writing of this book) that Rachael has said she doesn't want to see them over the holidays. I will support Rachael in this decision because she has the right to make the choice.

I would rather that they had played a larger role in her life. I used to be so angry and hurt by this. I hated the fact that they treated Rachael this way and embraced their other grandchildren. Looking back, part of it could be they had issues with me. Adam and Sara weren't treated as warmly as their other grandchildren either. It took a long time to get past the anger. Now I just feel sorry for them. They are the ones who have missed out. Rachael would have given them unconditional love. She still loves them but she is very guarded with those feelings. She doesn't want to be hurt.

Most family members have always treated her with respect and a degree of understanding. At times, she has been treated in a gentler manner but it always seemed to be in a good way. Rachael is very easy to love. She is gentle and has a big heart and anyone who is around her can see it. She is always honest and doesn't do things out of spite. I must correct myself by saying that under most circumstances she would never be vindictive or spiteful. It's not in her nature to be malicious, but she can hold a grudge.

Rachael has always had a special relationship with my sister. They have a very deep connection. My sister always treated Rachael the same as all of the other children in the family. There have been a few times when Rachael probably wished she had treated her differently. She always held Rachael accountable for everything she did.

My sister is the one Rachael could turn to when she was upset. Rachael has always felt comfortable in their relationship. She has always been able to make Rachael smile. I have to say that my sister has always been there for Rachael and me when we needed her support. She was my shoulder when I needed one to cry on. She was my rock and sounding board and she never judged me for the decisions I made. I'll always be grateful to her.

Adam's daughter is a very precocious child. She loves Rachael very much. In the beginning, to her Rachael was just "Aunt Rachael" but as the years went by, she began to pick up on Rachael's differences. Usually, there weren't any problems because they have always been close and Rachael has spoiled her rotten.

There have been times when things have gotten complicated. My granddaughter has another aunt who is only a few years older than she is. She could see Rachael's differences and treated her as another child instead of as an adult. I don't think she did it on purpose, but she saw that Rachael had a weakness. Just like most kids, she took advantage of it. My granddaughter would follow her lead and challenge Rachael's authority. We all know how the mob mentality can make us react in certain situations, and this was no different. Rachael could tell she was being treated that way, and she would explode with anger. Then Rachael would get frustrated and try to argue with the girls. That would be the point when someone had to step in. Rachael had to be reminded that they were just little girls and she shouldn't get so angry with them. This usually led to Rachael having a meltdown and we would have to go through the behavioral cycles. Rachael always wanted an apology from them, but that can be a tricky thing to get from little kids. I would have to try to explain the circumstances to all parties involved. They had to sense that they had hurt Rachael's feelings. I would always hope that there wouldn't be a next time, but kids will be kids.

I can't begin to answer why family members reacted in such different ways with Rachael. It's just part of human nature. Everyone reacts different when faced with a situation they don't completely comprehend. Sometimes I think people are afraid of the unknown. The old adage that you can't judge a book by its cover is true. Rachael is unique and sometimes she marches to the beat of a different drum. Once you open this book and look inside the pages, you will see that she just wants to be like everyone else.

I have high expectations for Rachael, and I know she has them for herself. I plan to continue to do everything within my power to make her dreams come true. I will do this because I am her mother and she is one of my children. I would want no more or less for any of my other children.

CHANGE AND NEW BEGINNINGS

Change can be difficult. It is especially difficult for individuals with disabilities. They crave structure. They also count on having a daily routine. When major change comes along, it can be very challenging for them. I have always tried to maintain structure for Rachael and to avoid surprises whenever possible. I tried to map out our future.

I was a single parent for several years. I never brought anyone into our lives. In my subconscious, I just didn't want to face someone rejecting her. I knew how her own father reacted towards her and I didn't want her to face that again. I put my life on hold for a very long time. I wasn't trying to be a martyr; I just didn't want to bring any more pain into our lives.

My plan was that when Sara graduated high school we would all follow our own paths. Sara would be going to college and Rachael wanted to live in an apartment with a friend. I planned to begin a life for myself. It wasn't until a lonely January night that I began to wonder if it would be possible to have someone in my life who could love Rachael as I did. The thought of it scared me to death. I had no idea how I would find such a person. The kids and I would come as a complete package; it had to be everything or nothing at all. I even prayed about it. I told God what kind of man I wanted and asked him to help me find him. I put that in the back of my mind and didn't give it much more thought.

I joined an online dating service. I thought that if nothing became of it, I could at least occupy my free time. I looked at it as a hobby to help pass the lonely hours. I had a very fulfilling life. I had activities with the girls, church, and friends. I just didn't have that special someone to share my life with.

I did find someone. His name was Michael and he was almost a thousand miles away, so it seemed safe. He was a single parent and we had the same views on raising children. It was refreshing. Before we ever talked on the phone, we opened the closet and let out all of our skeletons. I needed him to know everything about Rachael before we ever talked on the phone. He was curious but very understanding. He even told me he admired me for the way I had raised her. We began talking over the phone and the relationship blossomed from there.

I was nervous when it was time for everyone to meet. Rachael has always been a good judge of character and I wanted to see what her reactions would be. Everything went much smoother than I anticipated. Rachael and Michael spent some time together and got along great. He treated her with respect and they just clicked. I felt like a burden had been lifted from my shoulders. Over the next couple of months things between Michael and me grew more serious and a different life started to look possible. I had to worry how this would affect Rachael and what it would mean for the future. We were in Tennessee and Michael was in Texas.

Everyone had some time off around Easter, so I decided to take a road trip with the girls to Texas. This is an undertaking I never imagined doing. I packed two girls and one huge dog in the car and set off on our journey. This trip was not to be taken lightly and it was something out of character for me. I can't explain it but it felt right. Michael and I had to introduce our kids to one another and see how they would get along. If we were going to build something strong, it would have to involve all of us.

We arrived in Texas and it was a different experience. I can't say that it was a perfect meeting and that everyone got along just great. That would be a lie. The trip was intense and a bit uncomfortable for everyone at times. Michael's girls didn't treat Rachael different, they were just very cautious. They had been through their own form of family heartache before and were not particularly open to meeting us. The trip did solidify my relationship with Michael and we decided to marry and be together at some point. This would alter my previous plans for the future, but my relationship with Michael was something that could benefit all of us.

I guess you could say that my romance with Michael was a bit of a whirlwind. Just a few short months after meeting, we decided to get married. There were going to be a lot of changes. Rachael was not particularly happy about this. Don't get me wrong, she was crazy about Michael and I think deep down she wanted to be part of a family. She just wasn't receptive to the possibilities of such major changes. She made it perfectly clear that she did not want to live in Texas and wasn't going to quit her job. She liked her job and she had friends. Michael and I were facing a tremendous task ahead of us.

So many things had to be taken into account with Rachael. I had to think about what kind of services she would be able to receive in Texas. How would she react to the change? She would be hit with several major changes at once. She would be leaving her job, her friends, her programs, and the structure she was accustomed to. On top of that, she would be getting three new sisters and two new brothers.

I knew she would act out and have behaviors. Rachael did not disappoint me there. It seems we had at least a minor incident on a daily basis. There were a lot of tears and Rachael was adamant that she was not going to leave Tennessee. She would get her own apartment and I couldn't tell her what to do. There were so many emotions going on at this time. It was hard but I knew I had to stay strong.

I have to admit that it would have been easier for me to give in to Rachael's wishes and call off the wedding. Deep down I knew that marrying Michael was the right thing to do and that Rachael would benefit from having two parents who loved her. We just had to convince her of that. We talked to her about the positive side to having a big family and moving to a new house. I knew that financially it would also be good. The daily struggle just to keep our heads above water would be gone. That was just an added bonus. I wanted Rachael and the rest of the kids to experience what it would be like to have a complete family where the parents actually wanted to be together. In my heart, I knew it was the right thing to do. I believe God brought us together. This was the answer to my prayers.

Michael and I were married in June of 2007. I was still working in Tennessee, so I decided that I would try to split my time between Texas and Tennessee. This would also allow everyone to get used to one another in small doses. I also had to take into consideration that two of the girls were going to be seniors and neither wanted to change schools. We didn't feel it would be right to ask them to give that up. It wasn't going to be easy but we were determined to make it work.

After the wedding, we all began a journey from Tennessee to Texas. You will just have to imagine, we were driving two cars with four girls and a grandmother, plus a dog and a cat. Both cars were having problems with the air conditioners, and hot doesn't even begin to describe the weather. I was able to spend time with Michael's biological daughters and talk to them more in-depth about Rachael and some of her issues. They seemed interested but didn't make much out of it. It was a good time to bond under the heat of summer. Rachael did very well during the trip but she was ready to return to Tennessee and go about her daily life. Rachael was still determined she was going to live in Tennessee with me or without me. Don't get me wrong. She loved Michael and enjoyed having sisters, but she had her own life. Convincing Rachael that moving would be good for everyone was going to take some work. We also had to show Rachael and the other girls that they were all ours and it didn't matter whose children they were biologically.

We returned to Tennessee and life went on. Shauna, the youngest of our brood, came back with us. Rachael enjoyed having a little sister around as long as she didn't invade her space. I continued to work and we planned on spending several weeks in Tennessee and then traveling back to Texas to spend more time with everyone together. My hope was that the more time Rachael spent in Texas the more she would want to be there. This was not the case. She constantly reminded me that she had a job and friends there. Tennessee was good and Texas was bad. We struggled with this on a daily basis. I needed to find a way that would entice Rachael to want to go.

Rachael would essentially be giving up most of the things in her life that were of importance to her. She had her own living space, job, and friends and a routine she was comfortable with. It was going to be a tough sell and I knew Michael and I were going to be asking a lot of Rachael. We had to make her comfortable with the changes and assure her that it would be the best for her. We had to make sure Rachael was going to have a new life she could look forward to. On a daily basis, I tried to let her know that it would be good and that one day she would enjoy her new life in Texas.

Over the summer, I found out that the grant I was working under would not be renewed. My job would be ending in

September. This was going to change our situation. Should I go ahead and make a permanent move to Texas or look for another job? I couldn't keep the house in Tennessee open without a job. It just didn't make sense for the family to live in separate states any longer. The time was fast approaching and Rachael needed to be on board with all of the changes. It was not going to be an easy task. It was going to take a lot of strength and determination on everyone's part. Rachael felt as if we were pulling her world out from under her. We were. I was torn but I knew it would be best for everyone, especially Rachael. She would get to have the structure and support of a complete family.

We decided to make the move in August. I planned to travel between Tennessee and Texas until my work was complete. I wanted to complete the job I had started. I didn't look forward to telling Rachael she would need to turn in her notice at work. We planned to pack up the house and move everything by mid-month. Rachael was still determined that she wasn't going to move. She had behaviors and they began to escalate. I was trying to calm and reassure her on a daily and sometimes hourly basis. Michael talked to Rachael on the phone and also tried to reassure her. Another aspect of the move was that Sara would not be going to Texas with us. She wanted to graduate from the high school she had spent three years at, and she had a lot of scholarship money riding on it. She was going to be moving in with her biological father. This complicated the situation even more, but it was something that could not be helped. I still feel guilty that Sara was allowed to make her own decision about staying while Rachael didn't get a choice in the matter. With the help of Michael, I had to make the decision for Rachael. I had to do what I felt was in her best interest.

Moving was an experience. We hired a trucking company to haul everything but we had to pack it ourselves. The last night in Tennessee, we camped out on the floor. We had to get the baggage for five of us all into one station wagon and still have room for all of us plus one dog. When you are moving, you always forget to pack at least something, so we had a lamp and a few other items in the car with us. It was a seventeen-hour drive and we tried to do the majority of it at night. We had an uneventful drive until the car started to overheat in Arkansas. We decided to stop and get something to eat and let the car cool down. Rachael seemed to enjoy the trip and she didn't complain other than to let us know she was tired of traveling. So, this is how we relocated to Texas.

***

Rachael has always liked to be busy, but in Texas it is just a bit slower. Rachael had residency in both Texas and Tennessee; this would allow me to make the changes for Rachael as she transitioned from one state to the other. I made call after call to find out what agencies I would need to register Rachael with. Agencies are similar from state to state but they don't always offer the same services. It took a solid two months to make contacts and appointments. Working in the disability field helped me in the search for those services. I found that Tennessee was ahead of Texas in disability services. The programs in Tennessee offered more for individuals with disabilities.

During this period, Rachael missed her work and friends. She was also bored. She began to act out and tell me "It's all your fault."

Yes, I did make the decision for her, but it didn't feel good when she kept reminding me every day. It put a lot of extra pressure on Michael and me as we tried to integrate our two families into one. It was an intense time. As I mentioned before, Michael and Rachael began to establish a special bond. He was able to calm her down and she respected his authority. The behavioral episodes that usually lasted for hours were now ending in less than half of the normal time. I can't explain how he did it but trust me I was grateful. Michael talks to Rachael with respect and she has given him her respect in return.

Rachael went from having a busy and fulfilling life to just hanging around the house. She was frustrated and bored to tears. Rachael wasn't happy with her room accommodations either. She went from essentially having her own apartment to living in a smaller bedroom that originally belonged to her little sister. Rachael was out of her comfort zone. Because of this, she would act out. She was not dealing too well with the change. As I learned more about Texas Disability Services, I began to find things for Rachael to get involved with. Rachael was assigned to a caseworker who found activities for Rachael. This relieved some of the tension that Rachael felt because she was able to participate in the world again. She became involved with Special Olympics and the ARC. The ARC is a non-profit organization that provides programs and support for people with disabilities and their families.

Rachael and the other girls were getting used to one another. They had your typical family struggles. There were misunderstandings about personal space and borrowing from one another. Bonding takes time and I knew that it wouldn't happen magically. They argued like typical siblings who were brought together by their parents' marriage. The neat thing about this was that when they got angry with Rachael, it was not because of her disability. It was simply because they were angry with her. Her disability didn't play a major factor in how they treated her. Sometimes there were communication issues but somehow they learned to work through it.

There had been some major changes in the daily running of the household activities. Michael had a rotating chore chart that Rachael was added into. The other girls liked the fact they would have help with the daily chores. Everyone also has his or her own assigned laundry day. I think Rachael liked the structure and she did a good job with her chores. I will have to say that she picked up a few ways to cheat the system from her sisters. For example, if she has the tile floors, I have seen her sweep the dirt onto the wood floors that someone else was assigned to. It just goes to show she observes the world around her and is able to adapt to her surroundings. In other words, Rachael saw someone else get away with it so she decided to try it for herself. If it worked, she continued doing it until we brought it up to her.

Generally, the house is calm. However, like any typical house with teenage girls, there is going to be drama from time to time. Rachael has been an active and willing participant in the drama. There have been times when the other girls have been jealous because they thought Rachael was getting to go or do things they weren't. They didn't understand how Rachael would have money and be able to buy some of the things she wanted. We tried to explain the benefits Rachael received from the government and how it worked. We explained this during several family meetings. It wasn't overnight, but eventually the girls began to have a better understanding of the situation.

During this time, Rachael didn't have much contact with her biological father. He would call occasionally, but usually Rachael was surprised and would ask, "Why he call me now?" The calls seemed to leave her more confused than satisfied. I believe he mainly called out of guilt. I always made sure she could visit with him anytime we went to Tennessee. Again, it's all about structure and consistency. Her father's communication can be sporadic and when he does decide to call, it is hard for her to comprehend.

Rachael never had a good relationship with her father. She has long referred to him by his first name, even before Michael came into our lives. The relationship she has with Michael is different. She can sense that he accepts her on her own terms for who she is. As I mentioned before, they have a mutual respect for one another. That does not mean that they haven't had confrontations. Two major events come to mind.

During the first confrontation, I had to watch from the sidelines. Michael had to prove to Rachael that he was the authority figure and was the one in charge. Rachael was upset and had been yelling at me and was being disrespectful. Michael stepped in and told her "that's no way to speak to your mother." Rachael quickly turned her anger on Michael and began to yell at him. He told her to calm down. Rachael shook her fist at him and said, "I've got something for you!" That did not go over very well with Michael, but I knew that I had to let him show her he was in charge. He stood up and let her know clearly that she was not to speak to either of us that way again. When dealing with an individual with a disability, it is important for them to realize who the authority figures in their lives are. This helps to create the order and balance they need. This is why we made her sit and listen until she understood that he was not only an adult but a parent who must be obeyed. I was worried that she might strike out at him. She didn't. Something made her realize that this was part of the family structure and that she needed to accept discipline from him. I think that at that moment she understood that she was part of his family and that she would be expected to follow the rules just like any other child in the house. She immediately broke down in tears and then, as quickly as it began, it was over.

The second instance was a bit more dramatic. Rachael had been around others with disabilities in a workshop environment. She had begun to parrot some of their behaviors and we told her it had to stop. She got very upset and started yelling at me. (I always seemed to be the first target of Rachael's anger.) She was waving her hands wildly and getting in my face yelling. Once again, Michael immediately came to my defense. "Oh no, you don't talk to your mother like that!" were the words that he spoke as he tried to get between the two of us. Rachael's behavior escalated and she yelled, "I want out of here. I want to live with my friends in town. This house is ugly. Good-bye!" At this point Michael replied, "See ya." He was letting her know that that type of behavior wouldn't be tolerated by anyone in this household. I believe she thought he would give her an argument, so this just made her angrier. She walked out of the house and slammed the door. She went outside and started crying and screaming. It was not a pretty picture. Michael and I went outside to try to calm her down and bring her inside. She acted as if she were going to hit him and then she pushed past us and ran in the door. Michael yelled for her to go straight to her room but she refused. I tried also but she ignored me too. When Rachael is having this type of behavior, she always refuses to comply with just about anything. She ran back to our office instead. While Michael and Rachael were still having a heated discussion, I went to assure the other girls that everything would be all right.

Rachael and Michael were still in the office. All of a sudden, I heard a commotion. I ran in to see what was happening. Rachael had actually hit him not once but twice. He was shocked that she had the audacity to hit him. He did, however, recover quickly and told her to go to her room immediately. As he stepped forward, she balked and appeared ready to strike out again. He paddled her on the behind. That got her moving but he had to continue to paddle her a few more times down the hall towards her room. Michael was between the two of us or I would have done it. He told her to sit on her bed and not to say another word. She kept trying to get up and run out of the room. I needed to reinforce that Michael was to be given respect because he was the other parent in the family. Rachael needed to know that I was supporting Michael's discipline. I reinforced what he had been saying and that she needed to do what he had told her. I think it was at this point she realized that she was not going to win this battle. She surrendered and began to calm down.

Rachael needed to know what the boundaries were and what would happen if she tried to push them. I had to set the standard for Rachael and to let her realize that Michael and I are the parents and she must behave in an acceptable manner. Because we have expectations for Rachael's behavior, she knows what is appropriate and what is not. I believe that if we show her the boundaries and enforce them, Rachael will function better in society.

In my experience, children and adults with disabilities need to know their boundaries. They need the security of structure. This helps them to feel safe in their environment. Rachael has always responded better when she knows what her boundaries are and how we expect her to behave. This is true now more than ever because she went from being in a household of three to having seven people living under one roof.

Change is a part of life. It is as natural as breathing. There are times when accommodations are necessary. Accommodations can help someone with a disability to adjust to the changes. I have tried to instill in Rachael the understanding that change does not always have to be feared. Life is about change. Change can be good. Sometimes you need a good plan to introduce the change. You also need to let the person know how he or she will be affected by those changes.

Rachael then began to respond to having a two-parent family. She was able to see Michael and me function as a unit, and she is able to feel secure with us. The girls have formed stronger bonds. Now they stand up for one another and even cover up for one another. It is great to see the bonding that continues to grow. I don't have on rose colored glasses; I realize that as a family we will experience ups and downs. These experiences have taught me that it isn't biology that makes a family. It's having a parent or parents who show love and respect with boundaries and expectations for everyone in that family.

I expect that many changes will come in the future. We are a blended family still learning to function as a single unit. We have overcome many of the challenges we faced early on but I have no doubt that more will arise. We will all face it together.

RELATIVELY SPEAKING (PART 2)

The dynamics of Rachael's family have changed. In Tennessee Rachael lived with one sibling and one parent. Once I remarried and we moved to Texas, Rachael became part of a much larger blended family. She is now one of eight children in the family. This is an enormous change for anyone. It was overwhelming for Rachael. Honestly, I think we were all overwhelmed to differing degrees. We had a whole community under one roof.

The transition went better than I could have imagined. That's not to say that we didn't have tension in the house. Any time you have that many people living together there will be tension. This is especially true when all but one is female. We have faced arguments and hurt feelings but what family hasn't? I can say that Rachael has not been singled out or picked on because of her disability. She went from being one of the few to one of the many.

Relationships in blended families take time to form. Bonds are not formed instantly. In the beginning, family members tend to tolerate one another instead of bonding. We faced those issues and it was very hard for Rachael at times. She felt like an intruder and was out of her comfort zone. Her disability causes her to have added trouble with change. I took her away from everything and everyone she's ever known to live with people who were basically strangers. The kids only met once before the wedding. That meeting was not particularly smooth. There were a few bumps along the way. Rachael and the other girls had every right to feel apprehensive and even angry at the changes. There were times when they felt both but we made it through the initiation period.

It took time for Rachael to begin to feel comfortable in her new surroundings. I am proud of the way she adjusted to being part of a big family. She has shown courage and adapted well under the circumstances.

I would never have made the decision to uproot Rachael if I hadn't known in my heart that it was the right thing to do. It was not an easy choice, but I had to trust my heart and my instincts. When we first came together, we were dysfunctional individuals. As the puzzle came together, we evolved into a very functional family unit. Being part of a complete family is the best thing that has ever happened to Rachael. She finally has something she has longed for all of her life: love and acceptance from her entire family.

Rachael feels safe and comfortable in her new family. She has two parents who love one another and the children unconditionally. She has more sisters and they have developed a close relationship. She has new brothers who have accepted her without question. She is finding out what it's like to have a special relationship with a grandparent. Rachael has also brought something special into the lives of each new family member. It reaffirms my decision to join the two families together.

I am very proud of the way the other girls have accepted Rachael. They have learned to stand up for one another and actually enjoy spending time together. They have even found ways to overcome the communication barriers. They have spent enough time together that sometimes they understand Rachael's speech better than I do. That's saying a lot because I've had over twenty years of practice. I'm not trying to sugarcoat the situation, by any means, because from time to time the girls have issues amongst themselves. The issues are normal sibling issues that aren't due to Rachael's disability. As my husband would say, "that's a beautiful thing."

Rachael and her new grandmother have much in common. They love to go out, to shop, and to eat out. They also have a love of sweets. It is a match that was meant to be. Rachael is also very protective of her grandmother. She doesn't mind helping her and she genuinely enjoys her company. The relationship is beneficial for both of them. I am glad she has gotten the chance to experience this relationship. Both grandmother and granddaughter benefit from a nurturing relationship.

It's very hard for me to describe the relationship between Rachael and Michael. They accept and love one another unconditionally. Rachael has referred to her biological father by his first name for several years. She calls Michael "Dad." I get very emotional when I think about how she finally has this kind of father/daughter relationship in her life. At one point, I never thought she would get to have this kind of experience. Both Michael and Rachael have found something in the relationship they lacked before. I am so happy that he has stepped up and provided the guidance and strength she needs. It has lifted a heavy burden from my shoulders.

Rachael and I have a better connection than we did when we lived in Tennessee. We used to have a battle of wills on a weekly and sometimes daily basis. I have to thank Michael for acting as the buffer between us. He has a calming effect on her and it eases the tension between us. I am relieved to know that I don't have to handle everything on my own. Having Michael's support has helped to give me strength and to enhance my relationship with Rachael. I think I am becoming a better parent because I know I don't have to do it alone.

Rachael is happy with her new life and new family. It has been a journey to get where we are. Despite a few minor bumps in the road, it has been a smooth transition. It has exceeded my hopes. I can happily look forward to watching all of us grow closer with each passing day. Sure, there will be drama and challenges, but now Rachael and I don't have to face it alone. We have a family who will be there with us.

***

All family relationships are diverse. Some are more complicated than others are. Human nature causes people to react differently to family members with disabilities. Things that seam easy for one person to accept may be unfathomable for someone else. No two relationships are the same; they are as unique as snowflakes. I have come to believe that acceptance and respect are two of the major elements that are needed.

I don't know what will happen with the relationships between Rachael and the members of her biological father's family. They haven't made any effort to stay in contact with her. It's not much different for her than it was in Tennessee. I feel no obligation to force Rachael to visit them on holidays. If you don't have a relationship throughout the year, why pretend that you do during the holidays? In Rachael's case it does more harm than good. It confuses her and hurts her feelings. It's not fair to put her through it. I regret that I didn't put a stop to it years ago. I always held out hope in the back of my mind that they would one day realize what they were missing.

They say with age comes wisdom. Over the years I have learned a lot about family relationships. It has been hard for me to accept that I cannot change the actions of others. I can't control them either. I can only be responsible for my actions. I won't rule out the possibility of Rachael having a better relationship with that part of her family. What I will not allow is for her to be hurt by the callousness of others. Rachael can be forgiving, so if that is what she wants, I will respect it. That family was a part of her life and will always be to some degree. If Rachael wishes to renew those relationships, she will have my full support.

Families can be defined in many ways. At this point in her life, Rachael is experiencing a traditional family life. This is something she didn't get to experience when she was younger. Rachael's disability and the affect it has had on all of us caused a great divide within her biological family.

In our blended family, Rachael's disability is not an issue. It is just part of our lives. If anything, it pulls us closer together. Having said all of this, I must say that families aren't born, they are made. It takes effort and understanding to make the dynamics work.

Living in a family where someone has a disability can make life challenging. No two people will react the same way. Relationships will run both hot and cold. Overcoming the ebb and flow of change and differences will make those relationships stronger. Life is not always easy, but it's more fulfilling when you have a family that will support you.

Rachael's family life has taken different shapes over the years. She has lived with her biological family, in a one-parent family, and now with two parents and a large extended family. Through all of the changes, I have tried to keep her world consistent. Knowing that she has always felt loved and protected gives me a great sense of accomplishment. No matter how hard times were, I was able to provide stability for Rachael. It helped to form the person she is today.

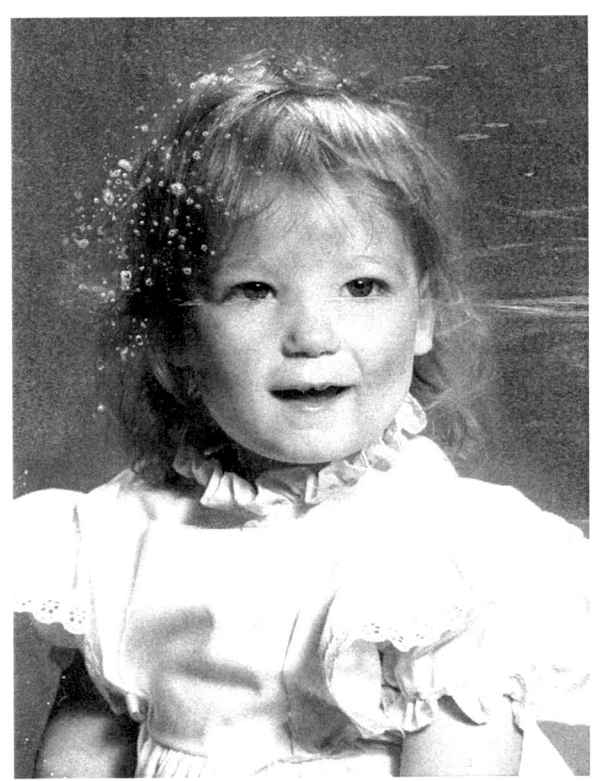

Rachael as a toddler.

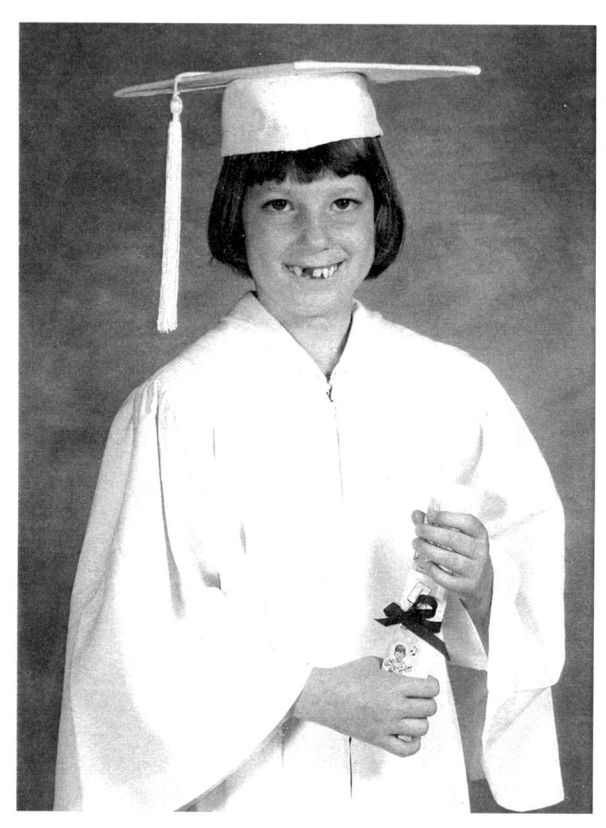

Rachael's kindergarten graduation.

Rachael's high school graduation.

Rachael, present day.

RELATIONSHIPS

Like families, interpersonal relationships can be complicated. Just because an individual has a disability doesn't mean he or she doesn't need those relationships. People thrive on human contact and the need to form bonds. It is a very important part of life.

Most individuals with disabilities are naturally open and friendly. When meeting someone for the first time, they don't have any preconceived notions. This can be both good and bad. They are naive and can be easily taken advantage of. This is why it is so important to teach a child with disabilities what is appropriate in a relationship and what is not. I have always done my best to give Rachael the honesty and respect she deserves when talking about these matters. For her own protection and safety she needs to understand that not all relationships are good for her. In the past, she has given people money or something that is important to her because she was asked. Someone would say, "If you give me your CD, I'll be your friend."

Rachael would get upset when she gave so-called "friends" what they wanted and then they proceeded to ignore her. Those lessons were hard for her but she did learn life can be unfair. I spent many hours trying to explain that not everyone wanted to be her friend and not every relationship is proper. The lessons had to be reinforced throughout the years because Rachael is very trusting and tries to see the good in everyone.

I have always found it better to be open and honest with Rachael. I would be doing her a disservice if I shielded her from the realities of life. I try to approach sex and other relationship issues in the same manner. Individuals with disabilities still have feelings and are curious. They notice sexual innuendos and have reactions to things that stimulate them. Just because individuals can't properly express their feelings doesn't mean the feelings aren't there. Because of this, it is more important than ever to be upfront and honest. You can ignore it but the feelings will not just magically go away. We can't go around putting our heads in the sand. As parents we need to be proactive in teaching our children. I believe we should be honest and explain relationship issues on their level.

You may have to take a different approach when explaining what is appropriate and what is not. Individuals with disabilities need to know about good touches and bad touches. They need to know what is acceptable in society. You wouldn't want your loved one touching himself or herself in a sexual manner while in public. They will be curious, and if you don't teach the right examples, you may see behaviors that are not acceptable. Remember, just because people have disabilities doesn't mean they don't have the same desires you or I do. Some people may not agree with me, but I think it is much better for Rachael to have a basic knowledge of sex than for me to try and keep it from her. For her well-being and safety, she needs to be aware of the facts. And if I don't educate, her she will pick up information from other sources that may not portray the proper lessons. The media bombardment of sex through everyday television and print ads contributes to the misconceptions of sex. If I don't want her to be misinformed, I need to step up and give her real-life answers. I feel that as Rachael's parent, I have a duty to prepare her for life the best I can. That means I cannot ignore the taboo subject of sex as parents of children with disabilities often try to do.

Rachael is at a stage in life where having a boyfriend is very important to her. I worry about what she might do to have that type of relationship. She is capable of love, so it is to be expected that she could fall in love with someone. At this point, she is enamored of the possibility of having a boyfriend. She hears her sisters and others talking about it and she wants that too. It is part of human nature to want love in your life. I have always tried to treat Rachael as I do the other children, so I would be a hypocrite if I refused to allow her to have a boyfriend. Besides, that should be her decision and not mine. If Michael or I thought Rachael was in danger, we would step in.

Yes, Rachael has a disability, but that doesn't mean she isn't capable of having a romantic relationship. Having said all of this, that doesn't mean that I'm giving the okay for Rachael to go out and have a sexual relationship. As Rachael's parent, I am frightened by that possibility.

However, I have to be honest with myself and accept the fact that it could happen. In the future, we may have to cross that bridge. I want Rachael to have the correct knowledge if it happens. I want her to feel comfortable enough to come to me or Michael with questions.

***

Predators are always looking for victims. Individuals with disabilities are often easy targets. This includes Rachael. She could easily be swayed into doing something she would not normally do. I have always tried to instill in her the awareness that she should avoid certain types of people and situations. I want Rachael to be as independent as possible, but I also want her to be safe. I can't always be with her to protect her. The fact is there will be times when she is out on her own. I want her to have the tools she needs to stay out of harm's way.

We teach our children basic safety rules. Don't walk into traffic, don't touch a hot stove, and don't talk to strangers. It has not been easy trying to teach Rachael she should not talk to everyone. There was a frightening incident when she was working at the movie theater. An older man was stalking her. He would show up at the movie theater and then he would find her in the mall. He brought a picture of himself and gave it to one of the ushers at the theater to pass along to Rachael. He even had his phone number of the back of the photo.

The managers took rapid action. I was contacted immediately and they alerted security. The man was banned from the theater and all of the staff at the theater was briefed on the situation and instructed to inform management or security if he showed up. Mall security was keeping a watch on Rachael and looking out for the man. I was scared to send her to work, but I knew that everything that could be done was being done. I did an internet search for sex offenders but the man wasn't on the list. I had a male friend make a phone call to the number and leave a message to stay away from Rachael. I had to trust that with all of those safety precautions in place, Rachael would be safe. I had to go to work and so did Rachael. We couldn't let this incident put our lives on hold.

Rachael did not initially tell me about the man but she did talk about it afterwards. He had asked her on a date. She told him she "not date old men." She asked him to go away. I have to believe that it is because I was open with her and talked about different situations, so it helped her when the man approached her. Her reasoning skills may not be the same as yours or mine, but she knew this was a bad situation. She knew what was right and wrong and perhaps she sensed danger. Rachael knew this was not an appropriate situation and she wanted to get away from it. I would hate to think what might have happened if Rachael had no fear of inappropriate situations. This is a good example of why I think it's best to be honest with your child.

Rachael has been on birth control since she was in high school. It's not something I wanted to think about, but it's another precaution for Rachael's safety. Rachael had a hard time with her menstruation cycles and I wanted to make sure she was protected against an unwanted pregnancy.

If Rachael was taken advantage of, I wouldn't want to add to the trauma with the chance of pregnancy. Before I took her to the doctor I even considered having her sterilized. I am ashamed to admit this, but I want it understood that I have been full circle in this matter. I had to step back and come to the realization that it was not my right to make that decision. I was thinking as a parent and almost didn't consider what she might want. It's not easy for me to say, even after all of this time, that I didn't even think about Rachael being part of the decision. I knew I could not always be there with her, so I had to plan for possibilities. It has been my observation that the more thought and work you put into planning, the more prepared you are for situations that arise.

Rachael has had many self-advocacy classes that taught her about her rights and what to do if someone tries to touch her in an inappropriate manner. We discuss this periodically just to reinforce to her that she is the one in charge of her body and no one else has the right to force her to do anything. It is important that individuals with disabilities know this for their own protection. They need to be taught that "no means no." Rachael knows she can express this by saying "no," shaking her head, or running away. Rachael makes the decisions about her body and doesn't let others force their will on her.

Social relationships in the workplace can be tricky. Rachael had to learn what kinds of behaviors are socially acceptable on the job. She had to learn when it was appropriate to shake hands, hug, or be in someone's personal space. There have been times when Rachael has had trouble respecting the limits of others' personal space.

I didn't want her to draw unwanted attention to herself for not complying with some of the unspoken rules of the workplace. There was an occurrence with an older gentleman she worked with. Rachael looked to him in a grandfatherly way, so she just took it for granted she could hug him. This made him uncomfortable, so Rachael had to change her behavior. I had to make sure she understood her coworker wasn't angry with her. At first, she didn't understand why she wasn't supposed to hug someone at work. She was hurt because she didn't realize why hugging wasn't appropriate. Rachael's job coach worked with us to reinforce what was acceptable on and off the job. Even now, if Rachael exhibits a behavior that is not acceptable, we can correct it by asking her whether it is appropriate. We use it as a verbal cue and to be a reminder for Rachael.

Rachael makes friends easily in the workplace and she enjoys the interaction with her peers. She has learned the basic etiquette for workplace behavior. We have been very fortunate because Rachael's employers have been very accepting and accommodating to her. I try to keep a good rapport with the management just in case any issues arise. By working together we have been able to help Rachael have a good work experience.

Communication has been instrumental in having a positive relationship with Rachael's employers. It allows both parties to make contact if any problems should arise. I have always felt comfortable enough to call if I had questions or needed to have Rachael's schedule changed. There have been many times when Rachael's employer has contacted me. It gives me a sense of safety to know that they keep a watchful eye on Rachael and keep me informed.

HABITS, BEHAVIORS, AND OBSESSIONS

    Individuals with disabilities tend to have obsessive habits and outbursts called behaviors. Not only do they have the normal childhood and teenage hormonal phases and issues, but they can become fixated on a subject or action. Sometimes the obsession can last for years or it can just be a phase. Rachael is no exception. I have seen many behaviors that have lasted years. There have been some that needed to be changed, and there are others that she still has today. I would only recommend trying to change things that could be harmful or inappropriate. It may come down to just choosing which battles you want to fight. If it is a behavior that is engrained into the individual, it may not be easily changed.

    Rachael has always been openly affectionate. She wants to hug and pat. Sometimes it can be inappropriate. Sometimes it can be very inconvenient. The first thing that Rachael does is to bombard me with hugs when I walk in the door. I know it is because she misses me, but there are times when you just want to get in the door first. I had to realize that I wasn't being mean because I didn't want hugs when I first come in but just needed a few minutes to unwind. If I tell her that I'll get back to the hugs, she is usually okay. I have learned not to feel guilty just because I needed my space as an individual, and Rachael has learned the meaning and importance of personal space.

Rachael still has times when she invades other people's space. It just takes a few reminders to make her aware of what she is doing. Generally, we just ask her whether that's appropriate. She says no and then it's over.

Rachael has always marched to her own drum but occasionally she gets sidetracked by someone else's beat. If friends or family members have favorite movie stars or recording artists, Rachael will adopt them as her favorites. When she does this, she goes all out. If it's a movie, she wants the movie and the merchandise associated with it. For example, she has a new Batman (*The Dark Knight*) lunchbox and thermos. She hasn't even seen the movie but it was a friend's favorite. It didn't matter that the lunchbox cost almost twice as much as the regular one or that she has two already. A friend told her Batman was the best, so it was Batman she had to have. She's the same with music. If someone has a favorite song, Rachael buys the CD. This can be an expensive habit and Rachael may have to give up something that she actually needs just to get the CD. I try to encourage Rachael to choose something because she likes it, but she often ignores this advice. I have watched her collect many things over the years just because a friend liked it. It's almost an obsession she can't quite control. If I try to interfere or end this cycle of behaviors, it just aggravates the situation. Do I have an answer on how to deal with this behavior? No. I don't and it can be frustrating. I try to deal with each situation as it arises.

Rachael has always been interested in music. She loves to dance and even sing. You may not understand all of the words she's singing, but she really gets into the songs. If she has earphones on and doesn't realize anyone can hear her, she holds her own concert. Music makes her truly happy. She can be quite obsessive about music. Michael and her uncle designed a computer just for Rachael last year. She had gotten an MP3 player for her birthday and wanted to download music. Michael showed her how to do it the first time but afterwards she did it by herself. She completely filled her hard drive with her music downloads. She could have probably started her own radio station with the amount of music she collected. It shows you that people with disabilities can navigate the web and use search engines to find what they want. Honestly, I didn't expect her to be so proficient at it but the proof is on the hard drive. Rachael is very determined in obtaining the music she wants. If she can't buy the music she wants, she will talk about it until she can get it.

One of Rachael's other obsessions is movies. Michael collects movies so Rachael decided that she does too. They like to talk about who is buying which movie next. It gives them something they can enjoy together. We try to have a family movie night on the weekends. I'll pick up pizza on the way home from work and we will have a few hours together. That's not to say that the kids don't have other plans. It's a hobby she enjoys and she keeps up with when the movies are coming out on DVD. She also likes to collect television series on DVD. This way she can watch them any time she wants. There are always movies and CDs on Rachael's Christmas lists. Rachael also likes to go to the theater and watch movies.

Rachael can also become fanatical when she wants something changed. She is persistent and she will not let it go. I mentioned earlier in the book that Rachael has a cell phone. A few years ago, our dogs chewed up the outside casing of her phone. The phone still worked but it looked rough. Rachael kept saying she needed to get a new one. I kept telling her it was okay because it still worked. As you read this, keep in mind that Rachael can have great difficulty when speaking to someone who may not be able to understand what she is saying. She took her phone back to the store where she bought it. She showed the clerk her phone and asked "What to do?" The clerk gave her a number and told her that if she had insurance, she could call and get a new phone. She brought the information home to me and told me what to do. I put the information up and forgot about it because the phone still worked. I was not in a hurry to have it repaired. However, Rachael did not let it go. She reminded me every day. Sometimes it would be several times each day. This probably went on for about three weeks.

Rachael went back to the clerk and asked him to fix her phone. He told her again what she needed to do. She told him to "Wait, talk to my Mom." She dialed my number and when I answered the phone, she handed the phone to the clerk. He told me Rachael was coming in every day about the phone. He said he told her what to do. I apologized and thanked him for his troubles. It wasn't Rachael's fault that nothing had been done. It was mine. The store clerk gave me the information and I called to order her a new phone. Rachael received her phone within a week and was completely happy.

I could have saved myself a lot of grief if I'd taken care of it when she first asked. It just proves that Rachael has determination. If something has meaning to her, she will make sure it gets handled. I'm sure it can be frustrating for her because she has to wait for assistance from others. If we ignore a situation for too long, behaviors can occur.

One of the main things she gets aggravated about is when someone doesn't understand her. She will get very insistent and keep repeating her words. By this time, she is frustrated and so is the person with whom she is trying to communicate. This can cause behaviors that seem obsessive because they will recur over and over until someone figures out what she is trying to say. It's not anyone's fault, since both sides are trying to reach the same goal. We still have Rachael write things down if we cannot understand what she is trying to communicate. It can be time consuming but it is important that Rachael be able to express herself. If it takes too long or if Rachael is in a combative mood, it can result in behaviors.

Communication is a key element. This remains true with Rachael. She has thoughts and feelings that she needs to express and her speech can hinder the process. Sometimes we have to try and keep her calm during this time. It helps to keep the situation from escalating.

Rachael is always obsessive about work. She has a wonderful work ethic. Over the years, I have observed that individuals with disabilities are some of the most loyal employees around. They are very concerned about being at work on time and about doing a good job. One year some family friends offered us a free trip to the beach. It took me weeks to persuade Rachael that it would be okay to take a few days and go to the beach as a family. She was worried that her manager would be upset or that she would be in trouble if she asked for time off.

Earlier in the year, she had to have emergency oral surgery and her face was swollen. Afterwards, she looked like a chipmunk. I tried to convince her that the people she worked with would understand. I also told her that she needed to rest in order to heal properly. Rachael was adamant about needing to be at work. In order to prove my point, I had to let her get dressed and I drove her to work. You could tell just by looking at her that she was miserable. I took her to her job and the manager took one look at her and told her to go home. I explained to her manager how I had tried to get her to let me call in for her and how she didn't want to let anyone down. Some people would have taken advantage of the situation and taken as many days off as they could. I am proud that she is concerned about her work ethic. A job gives her a sense of accomplishment and purpose. I believe her work ethic is something that everyone should aspire to. Rachael's concern for doing the right thing and being at work is one of the things that make her who she is.

Rachael rides the van provided by her employer for transportation to her current job. She has to wait at times if someone is running late. Rachael is not good at this. If she is supposed to be picked up at 10:30 and her ride is not there by 10:32, I get a phone call by 10:33. She starts to go into a minor meltdown. I can usually convince her to wait a few more minutes. Sometimes this works and sometimes it doesn't. Therefore, I start making phone calls to find out when her ride will be there to pick her up. She seems to be reassured after I talk to someone.

I spoke to Rachael's case manager to let her know what was going on. The service provider came up with a solution. Luckily, I have been taken out of the process. Rachael now has the numbers of the staff and supervisors who are in charge of her transportation. If her ride is late, she can make the phone call herself. This has been a tremendous help to me. I don't have to worry about having to tie up part of my morning trying to find out why Rachael's transportation is late. Now I only have to wait for a text to ask her whether she needs to wear a jacket to work.

Rachael can also become obsessed with people. When she was younger, it was with celebrities. Just like any typical teenager, she had posters and magazines that featured all of her favorite boy bands. She wanted to find out any and all information she could about them. As she grows older, she can become obsessive about her friends. She thinks anything her friends tell her is the absolute truth. This can sometimes lead to misunderstandings and even arguments. Rachael is a very loyal friend and she even takes on some of the characteristics of her friends. For example, she begins to like the same music, movies, and foods they like and even becomes interested in their hobbies. She can also pick up unwanted behaviors. This may be by acting out or it might be certain words she will use. Rachael seems to try to emulate her friends and their behaviors. She also wants to talk to them on the phone all of the time and then tell her family about them. It doesn't matter whether the person is male or female.

She has a habit of imitating the behaviors when she spends more time with people who have more severe disabilities. For example, when she worked at the training workshop, she would frequently come home with an unwanted behavior she had learned from someone there. She saw someone have a behavior without consequence and so she would try it at home. Unfortunately for Rachael, Michael and I catch on quickly and we try to discourage the behaviors.

I have taught Rachael that some behaviors are acceptable while others are not. Some of the things she mirrored from others were not appropriate. I think all children and young adults pick up habits and behaviors from their peers. Rachael can carry this out to the extreme.

Rachael has imitated the way someone talks or dresses and even words or phrases she has heard others use. She has picked up vulgar slang in both words and sign language. That is one reason I have tried to be honest with her when I have discussed sex and other subjects. If she knows the truth, she may not resort to using some of the things she has heard from others. Generally, if I explain why those words or phrases are inappropriate, she will discontinue their use.

There have been times when Rachael has witnessed outbursts from others and mirrored that behavior at home. When this happens, she generally becomes more physical. She can even be threatening towards others in the household. It's at this point that Michael or I have to step in and take control of the situation. Sometimes that means we have to keep Rachael at home and away from the people she has picked up those behaviors from. When this happens, it can result in tears from Rachael and frustration for all. It takes Rachael a while to understand why we have to separate her from the places she picks up the behaviors. We have to remind her that that is why she may have to miss an activity or event she was looking forward to attending.

I have noticed that she does not do this when she is working at a public job. She sees that certain behaviors will not be tolerated in the workplace and abides by those rules. Rachael's environment is very conducive to the types of behaviors she exhibits. That is one reason I have always been reluctant to have her live in a group-home setting. I don't want her to mirror behaviors that aren't acceptable in public. I have found that the best way to prevent this is to keep her away from those types of situations. Where she works now, being healthy is a big topic. Rachael has been working at trying to make healthy nutrition choices. This behavior will not cause her or anyone else harm, so I have not discouraged it.

If she develops a crush on a boy, she seems to want to smother him. I think it is subconscious; she isn't always aware that she is doing it. In the past, I have tried to explain that the girl should let the boy call her. Sometimes it works and sometimes it doesn't. It can be a thin line sometimes because Rachael has always wanted to have a boyfriend. I have to worry about what she might be willing to do in order to make it happen. I am so grateful that Rachael now has a father figure who will talk to her and give her advice. He also gives her the fatherly speech about what is appropriate and what is not in a relationship. Rachael seems to respect this approach. It shows her that we have the same expectations for her and a romantic relationship that we do for the other girls.

Like most females, Rachael loves to shop. I believe it is one reason she likes to work. She looks forward to the weekend because she knows at some point she will go to town. We have to set a limit or she would spend all of the money she has. Sometimes she has to make choices. She may want to purchase both a CD and a DVD but she has to choose. It is a good lesson for her because she has to decide what her priorities are. I can tell her "yes, you can buy a movie but you won't have enough money for your lunch." Rachael usually makes the right decision. Like all teenagers and young adults, she occasionally overspends. Sometimes she has to ask for a loan so she can buy a soda or snack.

Rachael also loves to buy things for other people. She spoils her cat and her niece and nephews. She is always asking whether her sisters have lunch money. It makes me very proud as a mother to see her generous nature. I do worry about her being so giving to people who could possibly take advantage of her.

As far as obsessions go, Rachael does have them. Sometimes I will take steps to intervene and alter certain behaviors. I try to choose my battles wisely. If the behaviors or obsessions aren't inappropriate for Rachael or anyone else, I will generally overlook them. Rachael is who she is and I don't want to interrupt her individual rhythm. It is what makes her who she is.

It can be hard at times to watch Rachael go through these phases of obsession. Most of the time, my hands are tied and there isn't much I can do. I just have to watch them run their course. It's fairly predictable that each obsession will be replaced by another one. As a parent, I just have to make sure she doesn't come to any harm because of the behaviors that are associated with the obsessions.

***

ACTIVITIES, RESPONSIBILITIES, AND RIGHTS

Everyone thrives on having hobbies and activities they enjoy. Individuals with disabilities are no exception. Rachael loves to stay busy and has activities she looks forward to. Rachael enjoys being out with people and participating in group events. She likes going to dances and the movies, bowling, basketball and other sporting events.

Rachael likes being part of a team or group. She has always been a very social person and group activities are a good outlet for her. It allows her to participate in something she enjoys and socialize at the same time. During Rachael's first year in Texas, she didn't work. It is very important that she interact with her peers. That is how she became involved in Special Olympics.

The first event she attended was bowling. We didn't know anyone there but it was a start. Now everyone knows Rachael and other members of our family. It has allowed Rachael's new family to see what it's like to be with individuals with disabilities. As a family, we benefit from being involved. Rachael also played basketball and took part in track and field events for Special Olympics.

It was good for her because she was forced to get off the couch and actually do a bit of physical activity. I was surprised that she wanted to run. She wasn't very good at it but she didn't give up. She tried and was part of the team, and that was what was most important. Over time, she improved and I think she actually enjoyed it. She now looks forward to each new activity. She enjoys the activity and being with her friends.

Everyone has his or her own little niche. Rachael's niche is staying involved in activities that allow her to socialize with others. Rachael has many different interests. Going to dances is a very important activity for her. She likes to dance and she loves to hang out with her friends. The first time she went, I couldn't get her out on the dance floor. Once she came to know everyone it became a different story. Now she has no problem being in the spotlight.

Social activities are very important. They provide a sense of being part of something and can give an individual something to look forward to. Before Rachael went back to work, her schedule revolved around her activities. It was her lifeline and gave her a connection to people outside of the family. Going to church is also a good activity. Rachael can learn and have fellowship with others. It is very important to Rachael that she remains in the mainstream of church activities. Rachael doesn't like to be in a special needs class but prefers to be involved with people her own age. One of her favorite activities would be going on to the Youth Conferences with the high school and college kids. They would leave on Friday and come back late on Sunday. She looked forward to it every year. I will admit that I looked forward to it also. Her sister Sara also went on the trips. They enjoyed it as long as they didn't have to share a room. This was the one weekend of the year that I was an adult with no responsibilities. Some years I made plans and other years I would just spend the time relaxing. Rachael's group activities benefited our entire family.

Things are a bit different now that we have a much larger family. It is important that the entire family feels involved and that their activities are important to all of us. After all, Rachael is not an only child. She went from being one of three to being one of eight. This was a huge adjustment for everyone. Michael and I try to make sure the kids have balance. By this I mean that we try not to play favorites and allow Rachael to be the focus of our attention. I realize that sometimes it may look as if we do, but that is not the case. We try to provide opportunities for all the girls and try to participate in their lives. If someone has a band concert or school event, we try to attend as a family. Sometimes they say they don't want to have a parent there, but I tend to disagree. Deep down all kids want their parents to be proud of them and to be involved in their lives. I take Rachael to their events and I bring them to Rachael's activities. This allows them to see one another in a different light and it helps them to bond as siblings. It is always a good feeling when your family is on the sidelines cheering you on.

Rachael also enjoys family activities. I try to include all of the girls in activities over the weekend. It may be something as simple as going to the grocery store, or it might even be taking a picnic to the lake. We also like to play board and card games. Rachael seems to enjoy being part of a larger family. I believe her sisters enjoy having her around too. They have started to conspire with each other and make plans together. It is wonderful to watch it unfold. It is very important that we go places and do things as a family. In our house, Rachael plays a major part in family activities.

Rachael has tried many hobbies over the years. Some she enjoyed and others she disliked. I have always wanted to give her a chance at anything she might have an interest in. That is one reason I wanted her to try extracurricular activities when she was in school. Sometimes you have to jump in and try it to see if you will enjoy it. That is also the reason I allowed her to try out for cheerleader. I had no illusions that she would make the squad; in all actuality I knew she would probably end up disappointed. I didn't want to deprive her of the chance to experience the facets of trying out for an activity. I showed her support and she taught me about courage.

During middle school, she participated in two activities she really enjoyed. The first activity was helping the librarian. It seemed strange to me that the librarian wanted Rachael to help. There were other kids better suited for the job, but the librarian gave Rachael an opportunity to try something different. Rachael loved working in the library. She felt important and included. She did a good job because she was proud of what she was doing.

The second activity she participated in was as the team manager for the girls basketball team. She tried out for the team and didn't make it but was offered the manager's position. She was able to be part of the team and she went to the games. She even had a uniform shirt just like the coaches. It was great because her little sister was on the cheerleading squad and this meant their individual activities were at the same place. I was able to be there for both of the girls and we made it into a family activity.

Volunteering has been an important activity for our family. My children have always volunteered me to help at school so I have returned the favor. Throughout the years, we worked as a group and if I volunteered, I made sure the girls were included. It has been good for Rachael to give back to others. As a family, we helped feed the homeless, painted faces at festivals, helped the elderly, visited nursing homes, and participated in many other activities. I think it shows that everyone has something to offer. They may play a large part in something or maybe just a supporting role, but the key is to be involved.

It is important for individuals with disabilities to be provided an opportunity to give back to the community. Just because someone is different does not meant they don't have something to offer society. Sometimes you just have to give them a chance. That may involve giving them a little extra push. I know that I have done that for Rachael a few times. It has been good for her to be involved in different activities. She has a lot to offer and having the opportunity to give back is very important. I have no doubt that she will always be busy and involved with the world around her.

***

Responsibilities are important to individuals with disabilities. They may not be able to handle the responsibilities you and I do, but they need to have a sense of purpose. I think it is very important that any child be given chores at an early age. The chores might be relatively easy, but they are necessary just the same. Children with disabilities need to know that they still have expectations within the family unit. This reaffirms that they can make important contributions to the family.

Rachael has always had chores. There were some things she did not do but she has always had to contribute with her share of chores. Just like any other child, she sometimes did it kicking and screaming all of the way. I would have been doing her a disservice if I did not expect her to do her part.

Outdoor work is not something I pushed Rachael to do. Since I was a single parent for a while, I tried to do most of the yard work myself. I would have Rachael pick up branches and things that ended up in the yard, but I did the bulk of the work myself. I actually enjoyed it and it allowed me to work off some steam from time to time. That all changed when we moved to Texas.

It was hard for me to get used to having a husband to work outside. He had all of the girls working and this included Rachael.

She didn't seem to mind. I believe she enjoyed being part of the family team. She did try to get out of work from time to time. She was "tired today" or "I'm busy, leave me alone." It didn't work. Michael or I would go get her and bring her back to the group. It was important to show her that she was part of the family and that she had responsibilities too.

Rachael got her first taste of mowing this year. I never thought I would see that day but I did. I was very apprehensive but Michael had great faith in her. We have a self-propelled lawn mower, so it is a little complicated to operate because of the multiple levers. But aside from that, it is easier to use. Michael had all three of the girls in the backyard training them in the basics of how to use a lawnmower.

They had to learn how to fill the gas and how to start it. It was funny to watch because none of the girls had mowed before. Rachael was the second one to mow. I walked beside her and told her when to turn and in which direction. In the beginning, she looked like a blind person trying to mow. That was okay because her youngest sister swerved just like a drunken sailor. The hardest part for Rachael was turning. She was all over the place. She got angry with me when I tried to show her how to turn. Michael had to take over. She had no problem doing it for him. She was tired when she was finished but she had a sense of accomplishment. She was experiencing something that I wasn't sure she was capable of doing. I have to admit I was impressed.

Rachael is working now and is gone the majority of the day and evening. Her job is physically demanding and she is tired when she gets home. Rachael is still responsible for her household chores. We expect it from the other girls and Rachael is no exception. It is important for Rachael to keep up with her responsibilities at home. Maintaining that structure is what being part of a family is all about. Michael and I try to keep up the example ourselves. There are many times when I come home from a hard day at work and just wish to do nothing. I know everyone is depending on me to prepare the evening meal. That motivates me because I know my family is counting on me. I hope we have instilled those same ideals and values into Rachael and the other girls.

It is my opinion that Rachael is a better person because she has responsibilities. She is accountable at home just as she is at her job. I think this helps to make her more independent and productive. My wish is that Rachael will be an upstanding person who knows right from wrong and contributes to society. I can proudly say that she has all of those qualities.

***

Individuals with disabilities have the same fundamental rights that you and I have. They can choose where they live and what they like, and they can even vote. I just wanted to touch briefly on this because we have experienced prejudice from members of Rachael's biological father's family. I have always taught my children to form their own opinions and to speak up for what they believe is right. Rachael registered to vote after she finished high school. Her biological father did not feel she should be allowed to vote and this caused an argument between the two of us.

Rachael and other individuals with disabilities may not understand all of the political posturing and debates. I have to admit that many of the things politicians say are over my head as well, but that doesn't mean I shouldn't have the right to vote. Rachael also has that right. She may make her choice for different reasons than I do, but it is her right to have a choice. She can decide which candidate she likes the most. Some may not agree with this philosophy but that is strictly opinionated. I feel that if Rachael works, pays taxes, and contributes to society, she has the right to vote just like any other citizen of the United States of America.

I will always want Rachael to have the right to make choices for herself. Michael and I will make suggestions but ultimately it will be Rachael making the final decision. It is important for Rachel to learn to make decisions on her own. If there is a safety issue involved, as her parents we would step in. We would never knowingly allow Rachael to make a decision that would put her safety or someone else's in jeopardy. As her parents we cannot always be there by her side. Yes, she will make mistakes but that is part of life's learning process. It would be wrong not to allow her to discover the right and wrong ways of making decisions.

Rachael makes her decisions when she is shopping. That does not mean we don't give her our input, because we do. We let her know if she would be spending too much money and if she needed to save more before she makes a purchase. I may have to remind her that she will not have lunch money if she spends more than she has. Ultimately, she will put something back and make the right decisions. The important thing is that she is involved and that she remembers that it is her money and her choice.

When making choices, it is necessary for Rachael to suffer the consequences if she doesn't make the right ones. Take doing household chores, for example. We don't pay the children to do chores, but they can be denied privileges if they don't complete their chores. They may be restricted from going to an activity or to town when there is shopping to do. I have to do the same thing with Rachael. I can't make exceptions for her because of her disability or because she has a job. Doing so wouldn't be teaching her anything.

Rachael wants to be very independent and treated "normally." In order to do this successfully, she needs to know that actions have consequences. It's part of the process of making decisions.

LIVING HER DREAMS

Everyone has a dream. Dreams keep hope for the future alive. Individuals with disabilities are no different from you or me. Rachael has dreams and plans for her life. Those dreams may change from week to week, but she looks forward to making them come true. It is my responsibility as her mother to help her make those dreams a reality.

I have always tried to bolster Rachael's confidence and allow her to try new things. It is similar to when she was younger and wanted to try out for cheerleader. I was scared and doubtful that she would make it, but I wanted to help her reach for her dreams.

Today she has dreams of getting married and having kids. I don't know if that will ever happen. The very thought of it scares me to death. I want her to be happy but I don't want her to get involved in something she may not be able to handle. As parents, we all wish that for our children. At this point, she has a boyfriend. It has made her very happy and she looks forward to seeing him each day. I think this has probably started her thinking about marriage and having children. Rachael is very aware of the fact that people her age are getting married, and she just thinks of it as a natural progression. In Rachael's eyes, she is no different from anyone else her age.

Many times over the years I worried about trying to push Rachael into following the dreams I had for her. I didn't give a lot of thought to what she wanted. My thoughts focused on how I could take care of her and possibly have a life for myself. If I had stopped and just listened to her dreams, we would have been two steps ahead of the game.

For most of Rachael's life, I spent all of my time taking care of her needs and the needs of my other children. I focused on what I thought they needed. I put my life in a holding pattern and used Rachael's disability as my excuse. One lesson I have learned is that I was actually doing her more harm than good. I should have been setting an example for her to follow and not playing the martyr. I believe I hid behind Rachael's issues in order to escape my own issues. I would guess that many parents have done the same thing. It's not wrong. It's just not healthy for our state of mind. Looking back, I can see that I should have taken the time to look after my own needs as well as my children's. I have come to realize I shouldn't feel guilty about everything related to Rachael's disability.

Yes, I have always thought that Rachael was born with a disability because of something I did. The doctor told me I carried a gene that caused her disability, but I still felt responsible even though it is something I have no control over. I still feel the pangs of guilt from time to time. Perhaps I may never be able to completely let go of the years of pent-up guilt, but I am trying. I have learned to just accept the situation and move forward.

It has been my experience that most parents who have children with disabilities have those same feelings of guilt and spend most of their lives trying to reconcile them. They tend to overcompensate and try to make up for their children's disabilities by bowing to their every wish. I'm not saying every parent is that way. But I have seen parents deal with their feelings of guilt by giving their children anything and everything they can.

It is not wrong to try and give your children what they want, but it is wrong to do it out of guilt. I know from experience that the guilt doesn't just disappear because you bought your child a present.

I am the first to admit that there have been times when I was guilty of that type of behavior myself. It wasn't fair to Rachael and it wasn't fair to the other children.

Nowadays, I try to make a conscious effort not to allow that to happen. It is important since we now have a much larger family. I want all of our children to realize that each and every one is important to us. I try to nurture each one's dreams but, at the same time, to treat them equally. This means that sometimes I may seem harder on Rachael than I am on the others. I have to watch this also. It is hard to walk the fine line between challenging Rachael and being harder on her.

How do I find a way to help Rachael live her dreams and pursue mine at the same time? I don't believe anyone has all of the answers, but I am willing to search for them. I have found that if I take care of myself and do not put my whole focus on Rachael, I am better suited for the task. Sometimes as parents we must learn to put ourselves first. A good example is writing this book. It has given me a chance to reflect and to think about the things I could have done differently. If I had known half of the things I do now, I could have made a bigger impact in Rachael's life. If even one person takes something from my experience that makes a positive impact in his or her child's life, I have achieved my goal.

Rachael has grown to be a very compassionate and responsible person. Her life seems to be going in the direction she wants. She has a job that gives her purpose and meaning. Her friends and family are a very important part of her life. Having a big family seems to agree with her. She feels accepted and loved. She has also found a group of friends she enjoys. She has started talking about wanting to live in a group home setting. She wants to live with her friends. I am not ruling out that possibility, but I want her to be here with the family as we try to strengthen those bonds. It sounds a bit hypocritical but she has something here with Michael and the other girls that she never had growing up.

Rachael is experiencing the give and take of being in a big family. She is learning about being responsible to herself and to all of the others in the household. This is helping her learn team building skills and how to share responsibilities with others. I think this will be invaluable for her in the future. She is also learning negotiation skills. If she does decide to live in a group home or in her own apartment, she will need those skills. She is also learning that the world doesn't revolve around her schedule. We can't just jump because she wants to do something. She is learning to work around a schedule that benefits everyone in the household. She has learned to be more patient and to work with others. If she ever moves into a group home, she will need all of those skills.

I will gladly support Rachael if she needs my assistance in helping make her dreams come true. I would do this for any of my children. It is a bit different with Rachael. Most parents of children with disabilities feel that they go through the child-rearing process blindly. We can only hope and pray that we make the right decisions. I also hope our experiences can help other families as they begin their journey. That's one reason putting Rachael's story out there is so important. It might serve to assist a family in making choices for their child. No two situations are the same, but people can gather information from the lessons others have learned.

Rachael is truly enjoying her job but she does miss seeing her friends. This is something we will have to work on as we go. I don't want her to feel isolated from her friends, so we will have to find a way to incorporate her social life into her schedule. I think she is beginning to understand that work comes before fun, but a person must find time for fun to have a fulfilling life. In her previous jobs her schedule changed from week to week. Now she works four days in a row each week. She is tired when she comes home. She no longer complains about being bored or about not having anything to do. She even has money she can spend. It is as if she has purpose in her life and it makes for a more well-rounded person. She is also proud that she now makes enough money to pay for her cell phone and to buy things for her cat. Her work group just recently received an award. She proudly has it hanging on her wall. This just shows me that even though Rachael has issues and needs assistance being independent, she is a very productive member of society.

DEALING WITH BEHAVIORS

How do you deal with behaviors when they become violent? How do you short-circuit the behaviors and stop the cycle in mid-stream? These are just a few questions I have asked over the years. Rachael has never been extremely violent but the potential has been there lurking in the background. I used to worry something would happen and I wouldn't be able to control the situation. Would I call the police for help? Would I have to put her on medication? All of these things are terrifying to think about, but it is necessary.

Rachael is a very sweet and loving person 99% of the time. It's that 1% that has made me worry about how I would handle the situation. Rachael is very strong, physically. I can never let her know I have been afraid when her behaviors start going over the edge. If I show fear, she will see it and that would make the situation even tougher. I will say I have been very lucky because Rachael's outbursts are few. I have seen parents struggle with how to control their children when violent behaviors occur. It is very hard on parents. Some are afraid of their children because the children are bigger and stronger than they are. The children do not know how to control themselves when the situation escalates.

Rachael has a very predictable cycle of behaviors she goes through when a violent event takes place. I know what the outcome will be in the end, but parts of the aggressive phase can be extremely frightening.

During most of Rachael's life, I have handled the aggressive behaviors alone. Her biological father was not a lot of help. He did not know how to react and that is understandable. They did have a few confrontations and it always ended badly. There were times I didn't know what to do either. During her high school years, things got worse. Rachael was frustrated and acted out. I also think the tension in the house between her father and me contributed to the situation. If I could have changed one thing during that time, it would have been the way I handled the marriage relationship. I think I would have ended it much sooner because when the tension lifted between us, it made it much better for Rachael and the other children. It is one of those life lessons we have to learn. I hope others will take away the thought that sometimes the environment our children are living in can influence their behaviors.

At times during this period of our lives I felt as if I were at my wits' end. I knew something needed to be done but I did not know what. I thought about seeking counseling for Rachael and the rest of the family but I didn't. I wanted it to be a family effort but it was very obvious this burden would fall mainly on my shoulders. I did not know anyone who had a similar situation, so I tried to handle it the best way I could.

I decided to talk to Rachael's primary care physician. He prescribed a medication that would help to calm her down and help diffuse the situation until she could calm down. I only gave the medication to her a couple of times, and I did not like the way she acted under its influence. It was a mild sedative and she would be in a daze for a long time afterwards. I used the medication as a warning. I would tell Rachael that if she could not get control of herself, she would have to take the medication. I understand that some situations require medication. I completely understand it especially if there is a potential for physical harm to the individual or another family member. No two situations are alike. Families must make those decisions for themselves.

There were times and situations when Rachael's behaviors scared me and others around her. Sara was very afraid of Rachael when something would happen when I was not at home. I had to work so I just couldn't get up and leave work to try and calm Rachael down. I did not want Sara to be in that situation, so I would tell her to lock herself in her room or the bathroom if necessary. Usually, Rachael would calm down and the situation would end peacefully. If I had ever thought Sara was in serious danger, I would have gone to her rescue. But being a single parent can make your situation more difficult. You are the sole provider and you can't put your job in jeopardy each and every time something happens. It's basically a judgment call and you can only hope you make the right choices.

My best advice is to seek help if you are facing this situation. Talk to your spouse, clergy, family, or friends. Check with service provider organizations. They may have suggestions for you. Seek out a support group. You can look for groups in your area or search online. It just depends on what would be best for you. Sometimes it is good to get out of the house and meet with people who are facing similar situations. This might not be possible in your situation, so you can try to find a support group on the internet. The main point is that you don't have to do it alone. Sometimes you need to have someone who will listen. It's okay to be frustrated and upset. Talking to other parents who are going through the same type of experiences can be extremely helpful. Support is a wonderful and amazing thing. It can change your outlook on the situation.

One thing you do not want to forget about is the other children in the household. Siblings' behaviors can affect them in many ways. There are support groups out there just for siblings. As parents, we have to make sure we don't put all of our energy into caring for the individual with a disability. We have to make sure the rest of the family is able to deal with the situation also. It's not an easy balance to keep. I have to admit that I was not always successful at this. This is also a lesson learned. I cannot stress enough the importance of being involved in some type of support group.

***

My marriage to Michael has been a blessing in many ways. His help and support with Rachael during her behaviors gives me such a sense of relief. His presence and relationship with Rachael have been so helpful. It has helped to take a great burden off my shoulders. It is comforting to know that I don't have to do it alone anymore. I don't have to try and be the father figure. He has a very strong presence and it is what is needed in this situation. Rachael responds to his authority. I do not have to worry about her challenging mine. After all this time, it is good to be allowed to play the role of only one parent. I can finally just be Mom.

That does not mean that I have stepped into the background or relinquished all of the hard issues to Michael. We work as a parental unit, and this is an important aspect of our parenting style. We support one another in all decisions. This comes across to Rachael and the other children in a positive way. I firmly believe unity among parents makes a big difference in controlling potentially violent behaviors. Rachael now sees that there are consequences for her behaviors. She also sees that Mom isn't the only one who is going to hold her accountable for her actions. I cannot say enough about the importance of parents supporting each other. In situations such as this, it is one of the most important elements in raising a child with a disability. Unfortunately, I never had the chance to experience this until I remarried. It has been a positive experience for all involved.

RAISING RACHAEL

As I have mentioned many times before, Rachael responds to Michael. She listens to him and accepts him in the parental role. Since the move to Texas, Rachael has had fewer behaviors. She responds to having a strong fatherly influence. I have spoken to my sister and other family members about the changes I have seen in Rachael. That does not mean that we don't have episodes from time to time. We do. Rachael will challenge Michael on occasions. This is no different from any of the other children in the house. Children will test the limits to see just how far they can push their boundaries. They may not admit it but they want the structure and those boundaries. This is true of children who have disabilities too. I feel that it gives them a sense of safety to know that their parents expect certain behaviors from all of the children in the household.

Rachael's behaviors used to last anywhere from a day to a week. There is always an underlying issue at the root of the behavior. She may be upset about something that happened today, three days ago, or months ago. There is no way to tell and we do not know what is going on until she finds a way to express herself. That is what truly frustrates Rachael. Generally, it isn't until after the tears when we are finally able to get to the bottom of the issue. Thanks to Michael's help, the process takes a lot less time than it did before. We can find the underlying cause of an issue in an hour or so. That is a great improvement.

Rachael is having fewer behaviors and I am less stressed. I do not worry about what I will need to do if a situation arises. I know I am not alone and that makes a tremendous difference. I was very apprehensive in the beginning because I did not know just what role Michael was willing to play. I didn't feel that it was his responsibility to help in these types of problems. As I look back, I don't know why I worried. Michael stepped in without question. He had no problems taking on that role in Rachael's life. That makes me glad that from the beginning I told him everything he needed to know about Rachael and her behaviors. I wanted him to go into this marriage with his eyes wide open.

That is something for single parents to consider. It takes an incredible person to willingly step into the role of parent for a child with a disability. When you decide to invite someone into your lives, it is not just about you. Because when you have a child with a disability, the parent and child come as a package deal. You really have to consider the future because there is the possibility your adult child will always live with you. In Rachael's case, she bonds with people very quickly. I did not want her to form an attachment to Michael and then not have it work out. Therefore, there are many things to consider before a single parent brings someone new into his or her child's life.

***

Do you feel that you have to protect yourself from your child? What happens when you can't handle the situation? Will you have to call in professionals? Some parents face these issues on a daily basis. I urge you not to face this alone. Talk to someone. Do not be afraid to ask for help. Many parents, including me at times, are ashamed to ask for help. I tried to handle everything myself. You don't have to go it alone.

I was lucky that Rachael's behaviors have never been severe enough to need professional intervention. At times I was intimidated by her and her behaviors. The situation was extremely stressful. It would have been better if I had sought help at the time. I might have found a better way to address some of the issues. Parents should never have to feel that there is nowhere to turn. Finding someone or a group you can talk to will not only ease stress but also connect you with people in similar situations. You might even learn a thing or two or, as I have, many things.

MAKING PLANS

Planning is something that all of us must do. As we get older, we start to think about the future. When you have a family member with a disability, you need to begin your planning as early as possible. There are so many questions to ask. The first question that comes to my mind is what would happen to Rachael if Michael or I were not around. It is not a question I like to think about, but it is necessary that we look at Rachael's options. I hope that with the proper preparation, Rachael will be taken care of if we aren't around. We have to face the fact that Rachael will probably outlive both of us. In order to protect her, we need to work towards making a plan for her future.

Whom would I want Rachael to live with if Michael and I were not around? That is a question I've put a lot of thought into. Asking anyone to be someone's support for the rest of his or her life is a big step.

There are so many things to consider. You have to consider what kind of burden it would be. You have to make sure your loved one will be cared for in a way you would approve of. As you are thinking about these points, you need to consider the fact that this will be a lifetime commitment and make sure that the person selected realizes this also.

I thought about asking Rachael's siblings. At this stage in their lives, I do not think it would be fair to them. They are just beginning adulthood and I think that having that level of responsibility for caring for Rachael might be too much of a burden starting out.

I know that if I asked them, they would do it. At some point in the future, we may have to do that, but I do not want it to be our first option at this point. I even considered asking her biological father. I don't think this would be in Rachael's best interest. We plan on asking family members who have already established a stable family life. This provides us more than one option.

There is also a likelihood that Rachael may want to live on her own. She would need to have some type of assistance but it is possible. She may want to live in an apartment with a roommate or in a group home. She has brought this subject up on more than one occasion. I think the attraction is living with people she knows. She also likes the fact that most group homes are involved in outings. I used to be totally against this idea, but I can see some advantages to it. Michael is not ready to consider this as a possibility. He is still in the denial stage. He believes that Rachael will always live with us. As for me, I'm not convinced of that. When all of the other children have moved on, Rachael may want to take that same path. For now, we have put the possibility on hold, but it will probably resurface in the next few years.

There is also the possibility that she may want to get married at some point in her life. Rachael is very interested in having a boyfriend. She likes the idea of being in a relationship. She sees the emphasis society places on the importance of people being in relationships and thus she wants it. She wants to have her own family. As a parent, I can say I am not crazy about that idea. I want her to be happy but I also do not want her in a situation that could be potentially overwhelming for her. As an advocate, I feel that she is entitled to make that decision.

Therefore, this scenario leaves me divided. If this comes up in the future, I only hope I can help Rachael make the best decisions for herself.

If Rachael did become a parent, she would need a large amount of assistance. I know she would love a child and do her very best to care for it. I just don't know whether she could handle the pressures and the challenges raising a child involves. You also have to take into consideration that there is a fifty percent chance that any child she has would have Pierre Robyn Sequence. That child might have more medical issues than Rachael. In my personal opinion, I don't think it would be in Rachael's best interest to have a child.

Nobody knows what the future holds but I have to begin to plan for different eventualities. Planning is always key. The first step is deciding about guardianship/conservatorship. I have struggled with this issue for years, and I am still not much closer to a decision than I was a few years ago. I have been to workshops and I have talked to professionals and attorneys. But I am still on the fence. I used to try discussing this with Rachael's biological father but he always dismissed the idea. I then came to the realization that if she was to have a conservatorship, I would not want him to be a part of it. I could not count on his support when she was growing up and nothing has changed to make me believe I could count on him now. Michael is more than willing to step up and be involved. He has said that since I am her mother, it should be my decision. He has stepped into the fatherly role and I want him to be involved. I know he has her best interests at heart.

I think the next step for us is to visit an attorney and discuss all of the available options. I do not know whether I want a full conservatorship, but I do want certain legal protections for Rachael. I want her to have the freedom to make as many of the choices in her life she can. I want to make sure we can protect her from others taking advantage of her financially, emotionally, and physically.

Rachael does not drive and I don't think she ever will. She may learn to drive in a parking lot or learn enough to move a vehicle if needed. I do not believe she will ever be driving enough to provide transportation for herself. She doesn't have the cognitive skills and reflexes needed to operate a motor vehicle. Therefore, transportation is a critical issue. Rachael will need to have transportation to and from work, to appointments, to the store, and even to activities. We live in a rural area, so public transportation is not an option. At this time, we have transportation to her job and back to a certain point. We still drive a roundtrip of at least forty miles to pick her up at the bus stop. Rachael spends approximately three hours each day just traveling to and from work. If there are any glitches in the system, Rachael has a minor meltdown. Since humans supply transportation, there will be times when the system breaks down. She has to depend on three different sources just to get to and from work.

When things go wrong, Rachael calls me to fix everything. It can be frustrating when I am in the middle of the workday, but I do what is necessary. It is important that I have the phone numbers of the people who will be transporting Rachael. Sometimes it takes more than one call and even e-mails. Rachael does not like to be late, but she accepts it much better if she knows what is going on. She does not like the unknown. As soon as I have an answer for her, I call her back. If I am not making fast enough progress for Rachael, she will call me or even text me. In the end, if I can give Rachael an update and let her know what is going on, she is generally okay with it. She likes to be informed. I have to say that if I were in her place, I would want to know also.

Now that Rachael has all of the staff's contact numbers, it makes the situation much easier on me. Rachael can take a more proactive role and can check on her ride by herself. It gives her a sense of empowerment and control of the situation.

If Rachael did not live with us, someone else would have to arrange and provide her transportation. This is something that must be considered when making plans. There were times when we have relied on her sisters to help with transportation. Rachael would chip in for gas and it usually worked out well for both parties. As all of the children go their separate ways, it will require more planning to get Rachael to all of the places she needs to go.

***

Rachael needs help with financial decisions. She does not know how to make correct change and sometimes she doesn't know how much money she needs to make a purchase. It seems to be best for her to have a bankcard. We have to keep a close eye on her accounts in order to make sure she does not overspend. This one element makes me lean toward having financial guardianship. I do not want her to be vulnerable to financial predators. I want her to have someone who can be trusted to help her with decisions that involve money.

I also do not want to take all of her financial freedom away. If she has money and wants to purchase something, I believe she should be allowed to make that choice. Rachael is a very generous person. She loves to give little unexpected gifts to others and she is always concerned that everyone has what they need. These are admirable qualities for anyone to have.

I have worked with Rachael so she will know how to budget. We talk about how much money she has coming in and what her financial obligations are for each pay period. This keeps her involved and gives her a sense of being able to control her money. Rachael is very good at making shopping lists for the things she needs to purchase. She maintains her cat's needs also. She informs me when she needs to buy supplies and this is great for me because it is one less thing that I have to worry about.

Rachael's cat is a big part of her life. I need to make sure that wherever she lives she is allowed to keep him. He is as much a part of her family as I am. This is something that will need to be considered when planning for her future. I think that when the cat passes away, she will want another one. He gives her a sense of comfort.

Rachael will always need assistance in making financial decisions. She has the right to be involved in the decision making progress. As her parent, I need to ensure that someone will be there to assist her when she needs it. It is an important part of the planning process.

***

Rachael is very healthy. Some medical issues will need to be addressed in the future. She will need help in making appointments and arranging transportation to the appointments. Because of her communication issues, it would be difficult for her to make these arrangements on her own. She is in charge of taking her daily medication. She informs me when it is time to reorder. She needs assistance in placing her order. I am working on trying to help her be more proactive in this area.

Rachael takes care of all her personal hygiene needs. She keeps track of when she needs to buy shampoo, toothpaste, and other items. It is a blessing that she can handle all of this. I do not have to worry that if she were in a group home she might have to depend on others for her personal care. She has done this for many years and it gives her a sense of independence. She recently purchased a battery-powered makeup remover. She used it so much when she first got it that her skin broke out. It took a few days before I figured out that she had rubbed her skin raw. She had to take Benadryl for a few days and put a cream on her skin. It's in situations such as this that she requires help. I do not think she would have known to take medicine or what type for the swelling. I know she was concerned and upset but she kept using the makeup remover. I had to tell her to stop. In just a few short days her skin had healed.

She still needs assistance in the kitchen. Rachael can assist with meal preparation but does not cook on her own. I believe that eventually she will feel more confident in the kitchen and begin to experiment. I do feel that she will need to have guidance in the kitchen. She will need help when shopping for groceries even if it is only with transportation.

Rachael can take care of her basic health needs. She will always need someone to help with appointments and ordering medication. This will also need to be included in the plans for her future. All we can do as parents is to take as many safety precautions as possible and pray for the best outcome.

ILLNESS AND DEATH

Illness and death are part of the cycle of life. It does not matter how much you talk about it beforehand, you can never be truly prepared for the inevitability of death. Some have a relatively easy time accepting death, but for others it can be much harder. It is no different for those with disabilities. People handle illness and death in their own ways.

Rachael has experienced both illness and death in her lifetime. Until recently, she experienced them on the fringe looking from the outside in. There have been people she knew or was acquainted with that have passed on. It was not until very recently that she lost someone who was extremely close to her.

Earlier in the book, I talked about the bond Rachael shared with Michael's mother. After the first twenty years of her life, she finally found the grandmother relationship that she had been craving. Unfortunately for all of us, Grandma passed away just before Christmas in 2008. Her death was very hard for Rachael. I think she feels cheated that Grandma went away so soon, but at least she got the chance to experience the relationship.

Grandma's health wasn't what it had been a few short years earlier, so she needed a bit of extra care. She could not do all of the things she had done in the past. Just before hurricane Ike, she had been visiting family in Houston and was forced to evacuate. I know she felt that she was a burden to us but she was not. Her living with us was good for everyone. I think she came back with a deeper appreciation for us as a family unit. I have to say I finally felt that she had accepted me, and thus Rachael was not alone in her loss. My role as wife and mother was now fully established within the household.

There were changes that would have to take place to accommodate Grandma's health. She was on oxygen full-time, so wherever she went the oxygen tank went also. She was experiencing other complications from her illness, so it meant that new challenges were always surfacing for her. She had extra medical appointments and she liked to have Rachael accompany her. They usually made a day out of it. They would start early in the morning and arrive home around dinnertime. I think it was a good way for them to bond. Rachael enjoyed helping Grandma and Grandma seemed to enjoy having Rachael to go places with her. They both received something special from the relationship.

As Grandma's health continued to decline, we had to make changes around the house. She required more help and everyone had to pitch in. Grandma always loved to have company and now she did not like being alone. Rachael had started working four days each week and it was keeping her very busy. She always made sure she spent time with Grandma after she got in. Sometimes they would talk or just sit and watch television together. Whatever they did, they both seemed to enjoy this and there didn't appear to be any communication issues between the two of them.

At the beginning of November, Michael and I had to go out of town for business. Grandma and the children stayed home. While we were gone, one of our dogs, Socks, died. It was very sad for all of the children. Grandma and the girls had to bury Socks. They all participated and had their own little ceremony. Everyone cried. This was the first time Rachael had experienced the death of a pet since she was very young. I think having Grandma and the other children around helped Rachael to get through it.

Shortly after our return, Grandma's health started taking a turn for the worse. It seemed she spent more time in the hospital than she did at home. I usually took the children to visit the hospital on the weekends. Rachael and the other children made sure we brought Grandma a bottle or two of "Perrier" because this was her favorite drink. Rachael hates hospitals and did not like to go there, but she did so she could be with Grandma. It was hard for Rachael to watch her as her health began to deteriorate. Rachael would not have missed visiting Grandma for anything.

At one point, Grandma fell out of the bed at the hospital and gave herself two black eyes. It looked very painful and Rachael cried when she saw her. Rachael did not like to see her in pain. Rachael wanted to know why Grandma was sick. She knew she was the same age as my mother. Rachael wanted to know why she, herself, was healthy and Grandma was not. Michael and I decided to start talking with the children about Grandma's health. We made a point of talking to them as often as possible and explaining what was going on with Grandma. This was to help the children, especially Rachael, understand what was happening and why. Rachael seemed to handle the situation better as long as we kept her informed.

The doctors told Michael that Grandma was entering the final stages of emphysema. She would not get better and eventually would be completely bedridden. This was not good news for any of us. We tried to explain to the children that this might be Grandma's last holiday season. We wanted to make it one that all of us would remember. We were already having a few family members in for Thanksgiving, but the rest of the family wanted to come and visit Grandma. The entire family tree decided to make it happen. We were going to be crowded and everyone would be doubling up in rooms, but we knew that this would make Grandma happy. She adored being surrounded by her family.

Grandma had to go back into the hospital about a week and a half before Thanksgiving. We were hoping she would be well enough to come home before the holiday. Unfortunately, she was not able to. All of Michael's siblings and most of the grandchildren were able to be here for Thanksgiving. We managed to sneak a plate into Grandma's hospital room. Rachael did not go to the hospital with everyone else, but she made sure Grandma's favorites were on the plate that went to the hospital.

Grandma got to come home shortly after the holiday. She needed constant care and Rachael made sure she stayed as close to her as possible. All of our children took turns sitting with Grandma. Rachael even slept in her room to keep her company. Someone had brought the flu bug with him or her and we passed it around at the house. Rachael was one of the unlucky ones who caught it. Even though she was sick, she did not want to leave Grandma's side. Rachael finally had to give up the fight because we were afraid she would make Grandma sick, which she could not handle in her weakened condition. Rachael reluctantly moved back into her room.

As November rolled into December, we started preparing for the Christmas holidays. We knew that the lack of finances was going to play an important part in our festivities, but we wanted to make it as special as we could. We planned to have a big gathering for Christmas that Grandma could enjoy. Grandma spent most of December in the hospital. Rachael and the other girls visited as often as they could. We always tried to be cheery and upbeat for the occasion. You could tell it was hard for Rachael to see Grandma that way. We took her a Christmas card and the girls made her a Christmas stocking. We hoped she would be home for the holiday.

On December 15, Grandma took a turn for the worse and the doctors asked the family to come to the hospital. We all went to the hospital except Rachael. She was still at work. Before the other girls went home for the night, Grandma had to be taken to intensive care. We decided that it might be better for Rachael if we let her see Grandma instead of trying to explain what was going on. I picked Rachael up from her bus stop and took her to get some dinner. I explained the best I could about what was going on. Rachael cried and we talked about it a bit more. I gave her the option of going to the hospital to see Grandma for herself or of going home. Rachael chose to go to the hospital.

I had Michael talk to her about what was going on. I think it helped both of them because they had each other to lean on. Michael walked her through everything as a father does and she supported him as his daughter. It was hard for her when we took her into the room because Grandma was on a ventilator and in a coma. She looked as if she were sleeping. We told Rachael Grandma did not feel any pain and that made it easier for Rachael to accept. It was heartbreaking as Rachael talked to her. She asked her to wake up and promised they would go shopping together. Rachael held her hand and told her she loved her before she left the room. It was a very tender moment between a granddaughter and her grandmother.

All of the family arrived later in the evening and waited. The next morning we left all of the children at our house and the grownups went to the hospital. There was nothing the children could do and we knew they would be more comfortable at the house.

Shortly after we all arrived, Grandma slipped quietly away. I think she held on long enough for all of us to come together so that we could support one another. It was a peaceful passing but that didn't make it any easier. I had the job of notifying all of the kids. I called the house and spoke to our oldest daughter. I asked her to take all of the kids in one room and gently let them know. Rachael did not handle it very well. She ran off and locked herself in her room. She just wanted to lie on her bed and cry. I called her and tried to console her. I had Sara call her and talk to her and even Shauna went into her room to comfort her.

Everything just went a bit crazy from that point. There were so many plans to be made and a constant stream of people in and out of the house.

Rachael wanted to go to work the next day. I think sticking to her routine as much as possible was the best thing for her. It gave her a sense of purpose and prevented her from just sitting around dwelling on the situation. The funeral was scheduled for the following Monday and Rachael was on vacation, so she did not have to worry about missing any time from work. Rachael's brother came in from the Air Force and I think his presence helped her. He gave her the additional support that she needed.

There are so many of us that we had to take two cars to Houston for the funeral. We were going to be meeting many relatives for the first time. I was afraid Rachael would become overwhelmed and have behaviors. I was very apprehensive about how she would handle the whole process. It was overwhelming for me so I wanted to try to make it as easy on Rachael as I could.

It was very apparent when we arrived that this was the concern of the other family members as well. It was a wonderful feeling considering the fact that most of them had never even met Rachael. I could not have asked for a more supporting family. They accepted Rachael for who she is and opened up their hearts to her.

All of the children were kept busy in a whirlwind of holiday activities that took their minds off the funeral and the loss of their grandmother.

Rachael went to the ballet with her cousins to see "The Nutcracker." She dressed up and had a good time. She watched movies and played games with the other children. It seemed that everyone did his or her best to put Rachael at ease and make her feel welcome. On Sunday afternoon, we had a big family dinner. Rachael did very well. There were times when things got a bit overwhelming for her, but she managed to keep herself together. She was a bit too touchy at times, but overall she handled herself very well.

The morning of the funeral was chaotic. There were fourteen people to get ready in just two bathrooms. Everyone even managed to eat breakfast before we left and we still made it to the funeral home with time to spare. The children all had a chance to see Grandma in private before the other people arrived so that they wouldn't have the initial shock at the viewing and wake. I believe that this helped them to get over the initial shock of seeing their grandmother in the coffin.

Rachael cried a river that day. Every time someone went up to the coffin and Rachael saw them cry, she broke down and cried with them. One minute she was comforting someone and then the next she needed to be comforted herself. I am very proud of the way all of the family stuck together and helped to support one another. Grandma's death was hard for all of us and especially hard for Rachael. Everyone came together and Rachael was part of everything. I have to believe that is just how Grandma would have wanted it.

***

I know that over time Rachael will have feelings about Grandma that she will need to express. Right now her wounds are hidden from the surface, but later they will creep up from the depths and make an appearance. It will probably happen when she is upset over something else that may be bothering her. We will just have to help her deal with them as they happen.

I truly believe that allowing Rachael to be part of this process has helped her to grieve. By approaching the subject openly and honestly, we were not only able to help her understand the different stages of illness and death but also ease her into the grieving process. I think it helped Rachael to experience this first hand rather than shielding her from the truth. I hope she was able to find closure and move on. I want her to remember the good times and not dwell on death. I hope Rachael now knows that death is part of life and that celebrating life is something we should do each day.

Not all individuals with disabilities will react the same way Rachael did. We must remember that each person will have his or her own way to grieve and handle personal loss. It is our job as parents to help them understand and cope to the best of their ability. We should be there to offer support and to help answer questions as they come along. You might be surprised by the inner strength of an individual with a disability.

Everyone handles illness and death differently. Individuals with disabilities should be allowed to grieve in their own way. All they expect is the same understanding and courtesies you and I expect, along with honesty and support.

BEING VULNERABLE

Rachael has a very innocent nature with a gentle heart. She wants to make others happy. She assumes everyone else is the same. I know from experience that most people do not operate this way. She is very naïve when it comes to trusting others. Sometimes it seems that we have to protect Rachael from herself.

I do not want Rachael to lose the innocence she has about her, but I also do not want others to take advantage of her. It can be very difficult to do. I have always tried to let Rachael know that some people will try to take advantage of her if they can, but she continues to look for the good in everyone. Therefore, Rachael is a prime target for being manipulated very easily. How do you protect your child from that? So far, I have been unable to do this. It is for this reason that Rachael must be in a semi-protected environment. I have strived to make her independent throughout her life. I have not taught her to be cynical or suspicious of human nature. Thus, Rachael will always need to be sheltered from those who would prey on her innocence.

Rachael's judgment can also be swayed very easily. She is a people pleaser and has an intense desire to be liked. She can easily be persuaded to do something if she thinks it will make someone like her. This is true of strangers and family alike. I do not think family members do it to be mean or purposely manipulative, but I believe they see it as a way to gain an advantage and to get what they want, as siblings often do. "You can be my favorite sister" is a statement that would easily cloud Rachael's judgment. This type of action from others has gotten her into trouble over the years. Just recently, her youngest sister convinced her to use her cell phone. She allowed her to make calls and to send text messages. It didn't matter that Michael and I had warned her before or that we told her she would lose her phone privileges. All that mattered to Rachael was that she was making her sister happy. Rachael seemed shocked when we took her phone from her. She knew that she was not supposed to lend the phone but she did it anyway. Consequently, even if she knows the right thing to do, she may not conform to the rules. She places more value on being liked and accepted than on the consequences of her actions. That, of course, may be said of many teens and young adults. However, Rachael will probably continue to feel this way for the rest of her life. She may never develop the careful outlook that comes with age and maturity.

Rachael is also very generous with money. She likes to buy things for others and is willing to lend money. Rachael doesn't like to see others do without if she can help. She would rather do without herself if, in doing so, she can make sure someone else didn't have to. Rachael spends a lot of her money on others. Sometimes it can be hard to convince her that she needs to save it or spend it on herself. That's a rare quality in this day and age.

This type of action just makes another good argument for conservatorship. If she can be so easily swayed by those she trusts completely, I have to wonder what she could be talked into doing by someone who makes such deceit a lifelong practice. A conservatorship would protect her legally from most predators. This makes good financial sense to me as a professional. As a parent, I still have qualms about a conservatorship.

One thing that it cannot do is protect her emotionally. Rachael tends to wear her emotions on her sleeve most of the time. People can sense her vulnerability. Unfortunately, you have to expect the worst from outsiders, considering that sometimes her own family will take advantage of it. I cannot change Rachael's nature nor would I want to. I can only put safeguards in place to protect her from those who would use her weakness to their advantage. When I try to discuss these types of issues with her, she becomes defensive and angry. She tells me, "I'm a big girl. You don't tell me what to do."

Rachael knows she has limitations but she is adamant about making decisions. If she doesn't like what I have to say, she stands up for herself. This is what I've taught her over the years. It makes me proud, yet it can also frustrate me. It is part of who Rachael is and I respect that.

Rachael also tends to respond to what others like and want. It goes back to her mirroring their behaviors and preferences. What everyone around her listens to determines what type of music Rachael listens to. It is easy for someone else's favorite to become her favorite. That is not just with music but also with movies, clothes, sports, and anything else you can think of. Since Rachael strives for acceptance and friendship, she wants to give gifts to people. She likes to buy their favorite things for them.

Over the holidays, we played a lot of board games. Rachael could be easily manipulated in the games. Michael nicknamed her "Big Money" and she responded favorably to anyone who called her that during the games. Everything was done in good-natured fun, but it is because it was within the safety of the family unit. Watching scenes like that reinforces my belief that Rachael will need to be protected from her own good nature. Unfortunately, I do not know all of the answers. It will be hard to do without encroaching on her freedoms.

How do parents do this in the least intrusive manner for their children? That is a very good question but I don't have just one answer. There is not a single method that works perfectly in every situation. Each situation is based on an individual and they can be as different as the light from the dark. I can only try my best and make adjustments when I make errors in decisions.

Luckily, I haven't had to intervene too many times. My feeling as a parent is once is more than enough. When Rachael worked at the mall, she liked to eat at the food court. She went to a Chinese booth to order food. There was a severe communication problem. Rachael only wanted lunch for herself but the cashier kept insisting she wanted four orders. Rachael was not able to express herself in a way the cashier could understand. Rachael paid for all four meals.

She brought them home on the bus and she cried when I asked about it. It was clear to me she had been taken advantage of. I was livid. I called until I was able to reach a manager and I explained the problem but didn't get much sympathy. Then, I called the corporate headquarters. This time I was able to get results. I smiled to myself as we ate those meals for dinner.

The next day, I took Rachael back to the mall. I waited until it was lunch–time and I approached the line. While we waited more people began to get into the line. When it was our turn, I asked for the manager and a refund. They gave me the refund and apologized to me. I told him that was not acceptable because I wasn't the one that had been taken advantage of. In front of all the other customers, they apologized to Rachael. I have to say it gave me just a bit of satisfaction to see some of those customers walk away.

During this particular situation, I was able to step in and help rectify the situation. Regrettably it doesn't always work out that way. By teaching Rachael self-advocacy skills, it is my hope she will stand up for herself when she is being victimized. She practices this at home. If someone takes something of hers without asking she comes to either Michael or me. She says, "I have issue." Sometimes we step in and then sometimes we tell them to handle it amongst themselves. Michael and I are there just to make sure the situation is handled without any mishaps. As with most kids, it doesn't take long before they are over it.

Hopefully, Rachael will use the skills she has learned with her siblings to handle other problems. I try not to interfere if I don't have to. I would prefer Rachael handle as many situations as possible on her own. She is more confident now and feels secure enough to take care of most issues that may arise. If she can't get a grip on the situation then one of her parents will.

***

Rachael is very fortunate. There are so many additional medical issues she could have faced due to having Pierre Robyn Sequence. I am thankful for that every day. Although Rachael has both physical and mental challenges it could have been much worse. I have often wondered if I would have the strength to handle more tribulations.

People always say God never gives you more than you can handle. Others say life is a series of tests. I have even heard it said that only those who are "blessed" are given the opportunity to raise a child with disabilities. I would never have chosen this path for myself or for Rachael. Even with its ups and downs, I would not have missed it for the world. I can look back at most things now and think things weren't that bad.

Rachael has brought many things into my life over the years. She's taught me it's okay to be different and everything in life doesn't have to be picture perfect. What matters is Rachael is happy, healthy and in a safe environment.

I've learned valuable lessons over the years. I've learned to be strong and determined. I stand up for what I believe in. I try to make sure if I'm talking the talk that I also walk the walk. Sometimes that can be really tough. On the one hand I want to react to a situation as the parent but then I have to think about what the professional in me would say. Sometimes I have to go back and analyze the way I handled a particular situation. Most of the time I do well but there have been times when I've fallen short.

I would not change Rachael for anything. Yes, she has issues and will always face challenges. She brings something into the lives of everyone she touches. There are people who can't see past her disabilities. They are the ones who lose out by not getting to know her. She is not perfect except in all the ways that really matter. She is a good soul with a heart the size of an ocean.

Rachael can be frustrating. There have been times when I would have loved to just throw up my hands in submission but all children can be frustrating. I will say Rachael does not lie, cheat or steal. She is always loyal to the ones that she cares about to a fault, even if she is not treated the same. That's just part of who she is. I can proudly say she is my daughter.

I would never try to take the "innocence" she has away from her. It is an intricate part of Rachael's gentleness. Her soul has a radiance that shines on everyone she comes in contact with. To me that means more than any degree she could earn or job she could have. Her light will always be there for others to see. It will not burn out or fade away.

SERVICES

Services are an intricate part of an individual with disabilities life. By services, I mean a system or organization that provides an individual or their family with something they need. Services can be needed for a short period or they may be needed for a lifetime.

Rachael received her first round of services at eight weeks. After she had surgery at six weeks, we were set up with an appointment at the cleft palate clinic. They would monitor her progress and try to address any issues that were caused by her palate. There were a team of doctors and clinicians from various fields who evaluated and monitored Rachael. The team was composed of experts in their respective fields. This is how Rachael was referred to other service providers.

There are providers for the many type of disabilities that affect our families. If there is an illness or a diagnosis, then there is more than likely an organization designed to help those individuals affected by the disorder. This can include service providers, support groups, medical specialist and therapists just to name a few.

It seemed that Rachael had a specialist for every part of her body and this did not include her regular pediatrician. We were sent to people who examined her eyes, her ears, her mouth, her nervous system and just about any other bodily function you can think of. I was amazed because on the outside, Rachael appeared as though nothing was wrong. I saw children with tubes and tracheas attached to their bodies. Many were in wheelchairs. At this point, I often wondered why we were there.

I am glad the evaluation team was thorough but all of these appointments took up a lot of time. I was lucky because at this point I didn't have to work. This allowed me to travel to all of the appointments without scheduling conflicts. This isn't true for many. I know as Rachael got older and I worked it became harder to keep up with all of the appointments. It can be tough on families as they try to balance work and family responsibilities.

This is the point were having a great support team comes in handy. It can be family, clergy or even friends. I've found it helpful to find someone has went through the same types of problems you are facing. I did not have that in the early years with Rachael and it made many things harder for me. This is one reason I have always tried to help other families. Service providers can refer you to support groups. If you still can't find a support group, form one. You do not have to meet often but it is good when parents can find a common bond. Often a few words of encouragement can make a big difference in someone's life. Sometimes we need a cheerleader on the sidelines to let us know we are doing a good job.

I can admit that as a parent, I still feel good when someone tells me I have done a good job *Raising Rachael*. It makes all of the sacrifices and hard times seem worth it. It makes me proud when others can see the kind of person Rachael has grown into and maybe I played just a tiny part in it.

***

As Rachael reached the toddler stage, she acquired more specialists. In addition to medical doctors, we began to see dentists, speech therapists and educational professionals. It became a full-time job shuttling Rachael from one appointment to the other. I also had a three year old that had to be tow along with us. I had to find ways to keep both children amused.

The dentists were perplexed because they just were not sure how Rachael's teeth were going to form. Her teeth had already reached the size of an adult's teeth. They weren't positive she would have permanent teeth or if these were the only set of teeth she was going to have. We spent a lot of time having x-rays taken. This is where I first became acquainted with a panoramic x-ray machine. Rachael hated that machine. She would have to sit completely still for about a minute while the machine circled around her head for a panoramic view of her teeth.

Rachael got to the point where she screamed if she saw any type of x-ray equipment. Because of the condition of Rachael's mouth, it was very important she have this type of x-ray. There came a point when we had to medicate her so she would sit through the procedure. Now I had to try and get a medicated toddler to sit still while the machine did its work.

Speech therapy was once attended weekly and sometimes on a bi-weekly basis. The therapists were concerned about Rachael's lack of speech. We began to add sign language in as a supplement so she could communicate in other ways than mere grunting.

The therapy helped with her oral motor function. It did not increase her speech output. We did find out Rachael had the physical capability to speak. That in itself was very positive. She was still was non-verbal. We continued speech therapy on a private basis until she was seven or eight years old. Afterwards, the school system provided speech therapy for her.

The next specialists we dealt with were the educators. Rachael was around four when I began to think about putting her in pre-school. There was a program on the Air Force base. She went there for a bit but the teachers were concerned about her lack of speech. The director informed me she might qualify for a program at the elementary school that was just off the base. This is where Rachael had her first round of testing for educational purposes.

The testing and meetings were heartbreaking for me. It was at this point I had to face the realization that the dreams I had for Rachael might not come true. It felt as if someone just pulled the rug out from under me without any warning. I was numb from the diagnosis. No one had ever suggested to me that Rachael might have mental retardation. I knew Rachael had physical issues but I never knew she had mental challenges as well.

I did a lot of thinking and asking the "what if" questions. Out of all of the medical experts we saw not once, did anyone mention the possibility of Rachael being affected my mental retardation. The diagnosis would not have been such a shock if I had been better prepared. Sometimes that's not the way life works.

From this point on, Rachael's educational career revolved around a team of educators. I was in the middle just trying to make sense of it all. I had no background in special education and I soon learned there were many options available. You just couldn't always count on the school systems to give you all of the information needed.

Sometimes you just have to get out there and search for the information that need. I began to truly search for help when Rachael was around six. I found out all states have Parent Training Information Centers. These centers exist to help parents find resources and learn the educational rights your child has. The centers are federally funded and there is little or no cost to the parent. Children are served from birth until the age of twenty-two. These amazing resources will place valued information at your fingertips. You can get information through the internet. You may also contact the organizations by telephone and request that information be sent to you by mail. Most of the training centers employ parents that have children with disabilities. When you contact them, you will be talking to parents who have had similar experiences to yours. Having this commonality makes what they have to say all the more important because they have walked in your shoes.

I attended workshops that taught me about Rachael's rights and how to navigate the educational system. I was amazed at the amount of knowledge I gained from the workshops. The more I knew the more I wanted to know. The best part was it fit my budget. It was free. I began to gather the tools I needed to talk to educators and ask for what Rachael needed. That doesn't mean I didn't face obstacles because I did. I ran up against a brick wall numerous times but I didn't let that stop me. I found ways to bypass the wall. To me "no" meant just push a little harder.

Other parents asked me for advice. They saw me go against the system and make progress. There were a few occasions when teachers approached me and asked for my help. Teachers are employees of the school systems and most of the time their hands were tied. I did my best to assist them or talk to parents they sent my way. However, I always tried to point them in the direction of the professionals. It was at this point I began to think about being an advocate professionally.

It wasn't until Rachael was out of high school when I was able to do this. It was not an overnight process. It took several months just to get an interview. I knew I might have the chance to help others. I did not realize I would have access to information that would be invaluable to Rachael's transition into adulthood. I could now talk to her service providers on an equal playing field. I wasn't looked at as just a parent but also as a professional. This made a bigger impact when I sought out services for Rachael.

Not everyone will have the same opportunities I did to advocate for their child on a professional level. That doesn't mean you can't make a difference, because you can. As the parent, you might have to work a little harder or have the professionals to assist you. Remember, no one knows your child better than you. That makes you an expert on what your child's needs may be.

***

Finding adult services for Rachael was a bit of an adventure. She was no longer entitled to anything after the age of eighteen because she has to qualify for any services she received. Luckily, I started applying for services before Rachael turned eighteen. Because she was still a minor, she was still receiving services under the law. This was a big help.

Once I began making progress, the process went smoother. A positive change came when I began to work for STEP. I made numerous contacts and had access to many different programs.

Rachael had many opportunities because of my networking. Many questions I had were answered just by making a few phone calls.

Many programs offer services for individuals with disabilities. They are interwoven into programs throughout the country. I would not have thought to look at Goodwill for driver's education. I was only aware of the fact they ran thrift stores. I attended meetings where their staff would come in and speak. I always learned something new and helpful. This is true of different disability organizations.

I now do my research. If I plan to speak with someone from a service organization, I find out about what the organization offers. I then talk to the representative to find out if this service or program would benefit Rachael. Then, I have to find out if she qualifies for the service or program. That seems to be the key issue. First she must qualify and then there must be a funding source to help pay for the service. That can mean she must qualify through both the program and for the funding source.

Yes, it can be time consuming. This process comes with a major amount of paperwork. Many times, we have encountered waiting lists. Sometimes you can be on a waiting list for years. Patience is a good coping skill to have when dealing with adult services because qualifying for adult services is a never-ending process. You must consider many factors when applying for services.

Finances are a very important part of qualifying for services. Until Rachael turned eighteen, everything was based on my income. Afterwards, Rachael's income was the basis for qualifying for a program. This is very important. Many families can only work for lower wages in order to assure their child can qualify for services. I have been in that boat myself. It did not seem fair. I have turned down jobs in the past because I would have made too much money. The extra income would not have paid for services Rachael needed. It is nice change now that the services are based on Rachael's income.

Age is another factor in qualifying for services. There are various programs for individuals based on age. Many are for those who are younger and others are for those who are older. One major problem for Rachael has been regarding dental services. Once she reached eighteen, she no longer qualified for the dental care services. My dental insurance would not cover her because of her pre-existing condition.

Some services are hard to obtain if the disability is sustained after the age of seventeen. The types of services an individual receives can be affected by the age the disability began. An example would be if an individual suffered a traumatic brain injury in their mid twenties.

Where an individual lives can also play an important role in the type of services an individual receives. Transportation is a very good example of this. When Rachael started working, I made sure I lived within the city limits. This allowed us to have access to public transportation which would pick her up at our front door. Thus, Rachael would have transportation to and from work. That isn't the case now. We live in a rural town that is at least twenty something miles from the city and public transportation. That is why Rachael depends on three different sources to get her to and from her job. She spends at least three hours each day commuting to and from work.

Where an individual lives can also determine what federal and state services are available for an individual. I noticed a big change in what was available when we moved from Tennessee to Texas. Many services and opportunities Rachael received in Tennessee were not available for her in Texas. Either she has not been a resident long enough or the services do not exist. That is a major reason to look at what is available in a state before you plan a major move. In Rachael's case, it was not an option. Our new family lived in Texas and that was where we were moving.

Socialization is an important part of adult services. Because the individuals are no longer in an educational environment, they may not have access to socialize and have activities with friends.

Friends and activities play a big role in Rachael's life. She is a social butterfly and loves to be amongst people. Since our move to Texas the ARC (Association of Retarded Citizens) and Special Olympics have provided opportunities for her. This was her world until she was able to find a job. The activities and being with friends gave her something to look forward to each week.

Adult services vary from state to state and region to region. There are many considerations to make when deciding what to apply for and when to apply. My advice is to seek out groups and individuals who may have an inside track to what is available in your area. Start with your case manager. He or she will have access to numerous types of groups and services. You can also talk with other parents. Parents can hold a wealth of knowledge about what exists in your area.

Rachael will always need to have assistance from adult services. Her needs are few at this time but as she grows older that may change. I try to stay current on what is available. This will allow her a chance to experience more opportunities as they become available.

HAPPY ENDINGS

I have devoted the past twenty-three years of my life to raising a happy, healthy and productive individual. The path has been interesting to say the least. Together Rachael and I have faced times both good times and bad. Today, I can say we are at a good place in life. We both have the love and support we have always wanted.

I am a better person for being Rachael's mother. I have an inner strength I never knew existed. I know how to appreciate someone for who they are and not for whom I thought they could have been. I have found beauty isn't just on the outside it dwells within a person's soul. It's not about what you have. It is more about how you look at the things you do have. Rachael's outlook on life has taught me all of this and much more.

Rachael has always set goals for herself. Today she has fulfilled most of those goals. She has a job she enjoys and it pays her well. She has a cell phone with a built-in camera. She has a bank card and money to shop with. She has her cat. (He follows her around as if he were a puppy.) Rachael has a loving and supporting family. She has many friends including a boyfriend.

The only goal she talks about is living in her own apartment or with friends. At this point, her parents aren't ready. We would like to have a few more years with her at home. It may be a different story as our nest empties. I still have mixed feelings and can give reasons for both her living with Michael and I or in a different environment. We may let her try it without us at some point just to see if that's what she really wants. We all know sometimes the grass looks much greener somewhere else.

Rachael constantly changes her mind about where she wants to live. She is beginning to understand she has much more freedom than many of her friends. She can be spontaneous and decide she wants to do something at the last minute. She doesn't have to wait on paperwork and approval from a case manager or staff. Rachael likes the independence she has at home. She does just about whatever she wants. She doesn't have a set schedule except one of her own making. At this time she will remain at home with her family.

Rachael has accomplished so much in her lifetime. I look forward to being part of her new adventures. Her path has not always been smooth but there have been positives we have experienced during her life. There are a few things I would have handled differently over the years but our experiences have made us who we are. Our situation could have been much worse. I am always thankful when I think back on the prospect of how Rachael's life could have turned out. When all is said and done, Rachael has a good life.

I will always be an active part of Rachael's life. Together with our family we will face any new challenges that happen to" come our way. We will walk the path that will hopefully take us to the happily ever after.

COMMON Q&A

Disabilities come in all shapes and sizes. Some are visible to the naked eye and others are hidden. The disability can be as unique as the person that is affected by it. Many disabilities are life-threatening and others will stay with your child the rest of his or her natural life. Over the years, many treatments and therapies have emerged to help our children live better and longer lives. As it stands today, disabilities can drastically affect the child and the entire family. It all begins when we receive that first diagnosis.

THE DIAGNOSIS
Learning your child has a disability can initially be devastating. You must go through the grieving process before you reach acceptance. Each parent must find the strength needed to go forward and deal with the circumstances dealt to their family. Once the original shock has worn off, it is time to pick up the pieces and begin the journey. The journey is a process that will continue throughout your child's life. It's not a game and we cannot take a time out nor have a do over. Life doesn't work that way. Your family will face highs and lows. All of the dreams that you had for your child will be changing. That does not mean that the journey will not be rewarding. You as a parent will experience

moments when you want to scream, cry and even laugh. Yes, I did say laugh. There are many joys that come from raising a child with a disability. The journey can hold many surprises along the way. Your family's journey is what you make of it.

WHAT DO YOU DO AFTER YOUR CHILD HAS BEEN DIAGNOSED?

Research and learn as much as possible about the disability. Do an internet search and visit your local library.

Find an organization that specializes in the disability. Establish contact and become familiar with what services the organization offers.

Keep a notebook. Compile all of the information that you can find on the subject.

Find parents that are facing similar situations. You may benefit greatly from their experience.

WHAT DO YOU DO WHEN THE GOING GETS TOUGH?

Find support. Look for a group or individual that will be your cheerleader when you need it most.

Take time for yourself. Remember you cannot give your best to your child unless you care for yourself first.

Ask a family member or friend to help out even if it's just to get a much needed thirty minute nap or to finish an entire cup of coffee uninterrupted.

Try faith. You can find strength from your clergy or community.

Laugh and do it often. Try not to worry about the small stuff because just like dirty laundry it will always be there.

HOW DO YOU MOVE FORWARD?

Change your outlook. Your child's life is not going to be what you may have wanted but that doesn't mean that life is over.

Re-visit the goals and expectations that you have for your child. You will have to do some adjusting but that's okay.

Believe. Your child can have a future and you will play an important role in it.

Plan. Begin to plan for the future and find out what supports you will need to put the plan into action.

HOW DO I KNOW WHAT TO EXPECT?

Talk to the experts. This will require you talking to professionals and other parents.

Be prepared to make changes. Many times things don't go as we planned so always have a backup plan. Life is full of unexpected events.

HOW DO WE COPE AS A FAMILY?

Talk to one another. Have open communication and be honest. Talk about your true feelings.

Seek support as a family. You can turn to your church for support or you may need to seek help from a professional counselor.

Don't overlook other family members. Children without disabilities can sometimes feel resentful because you are focusing all of your energy on the child with the diagnosis.

Be proactive. Try to meet any problems head on.

Remember to have fun.

Having a child with the diagnosis of a disability can be life – altering. This is the beginning of a new phase of your existence as a family. Staying strong and finding ways to accept the situation will help fortify your family. A diagnosis may be the end of one dream but it can also be the beginning of a new one.

EARLY CHILDHOOD

Early Childhood is anytime between birth and the age when your child is scheduled to begin public education. This is a very important time in the development of your child both mentally and physically. At this time, the professionals begin to gauge the milestones that your child reaches. As a parent you will see where your child is developmentally compared to others his or her age.

1. WHAT SHOULD I DO IF I SUSPECT A PROBLEM?

Talk to your pediatrician and schedule an appointment to talk about the situation.

Document. Keep a notebook or journal chronicling any issues that might cause you to suspect any problems.

Remember, you are an expert on your child. You provide the daily care, your observations are important.

Research the problem.

2. ARE THERE PROGRAMS THAT CAN HELP MY CHILD? CAN I AFFORD THEM?

Yes. Services vary from state to state. Find information on the early childhood intervention programs in your local area.

Contact your health insurance carrier to find out if they offer any programs.

Contact your local education agency or school system. Ask for information on their early" childhood development programs.

There are many services available that are free or of little expense to the parents. If money is an issue, ask about free or low cost assistance. That will give you one less problem to be worried about.

3. WHAT IF I AM GETTING THE RUN AROUND?

Contact your local Parent Training Information Center. Each state will have its own organization. If you have trouble locating the organization, contact your local education agency and ask for contact information for the organization.

Learn. Go to workshops and training classes for parents. The trainings are designed to teach parents about the child's rights within the educational system. Most of the workshops will be at no cost to the parents.

Speak to other parents. Parents have firsthand knowledge and experience.

Early childhood is an important developmental period for your child. If you suspect your child is not meeting the developmental milestones as scheduled, check with your pediatrician and the local education agency. They can offer you assistance if your child qualifies for an early intervention program. Do not be afraid to ask. You will only be helping your child.

EDUCATION

Your children will spend a major portion of his or her life in the educational system. A child with a disability can stay in school until the age of twenty-two. Your child is entitled to have a free and appropriate public education. There are federally appointed groups to ensure those opportunities are available to your child. It is your responsibility as a parent to learn what your child is entitled to and to make sure that he or she is given that opportunity. The state and federal governments have set up organizations whose sole purpose is to help parents learn about their children's rights.

HOW DO I KNOW WHAT MY CHILD IS ENTITLED TO?

It is your job as the parent to learn what services are available.

Check with the Parent Training Information Centers in your state. They are federally funded to help parents learn about their child's rights.

Attend workshops that will teach you about your child's educational rights. Most of the workshops are at little or no cost to the parent.

Visit websites that provide information on federal educational law.

HOW DO I ATTEND A MEETING AT MY CHILD'S SCHOOL WITHOUT BEING INTIMIDATED BY PROFESSIONALS?

Always remember that you are the subject matter expert when it comes to your child. No one knows your child better than you.

Take someone to the meeting with you. There is security in numbers and it is always good to have support in your corner.

Bring a picture of your child to the meeting. Make sure that every staff member there sees the picture and realizes this is who the meeting is about. This will help them realize that you are talking about a person and not just a name or number.

Take a snack for everyone to share at the meeting. This is a gesture of goodwill on your part. School officials generally react positively to this type of gesture.

HOW DO I FIGHT FOR MY CHILD'S RIGHTS?

Documentation is very important. Document everything. This includes phone calls, letters, meetings, casual conversations and anything of relevance. Keep the information in a notebook. Always have access to the notebook if you need to review any information.

Request help. Ask a professional or paraprofessional advocate for assistance. Many are available at little or no cost to the parent.

Talk to other parents. They may have experience and valuable information that relate to your situation.

Educate yourself. Learn the policies and procedures within your school system. Find out how to properly follow the chain of command when filing a complaint.

HOW DO YOU HAVE A SUCCESFUL RELATIONSHIP WITH MY CHILD'S SCHOOL SYSTEM?

Be positive and learn to work collaboratively together with the school system. Remember that both you and the school system have an important role in the process of educating your child.

Learn to be flexible. Your relationship with your child's school will be a give and take adventure. You must understand that you will not always get everything that you ask for. It is best to be prepared for that reality.

Communicate. The biggest problem between parents and school systems is the lack of open and honest communication. Parents and schools must work together in order to achieve positive results.

Education is a major part of your child's life. Learning to navigate the school system is an important step in your child having a successful educational journey. Be open to compromise because you will not win every battle. There are professionals that can assist you in working with the school systems. You are not alone. A good system of communication is the key to a successful relationship with the school organization. Remember that being knowledgeable about the laws that concern your child's educational rights is extremely important. By being proactive, your child has a better chance of achieving an appropriate education.

TRANSITION

Transition begins around the age of fourteen. It is around this time that you need to begin planning for your child's future after high school. You need to figure out what goals your child would like to achieve after graduation. After deciding on the goals, you need to find out how to make those goals come to fruition. Proper planning is the key to having a positive transition.

WHAT DOES TRANSITION PLANNING INCLUDE?

You will be planning the path that your child will take after high school. Your child may choose post-secondary education, vocational training or going to work.

Transition planning should include goals to help your child reach positive outcomes after graduation. In other words, the goals must help your child to achieve the path he or she has chosen.

The planning process should include where your child is now and everything it will take to get him or her where they want to be after they have completed school. You need what you want to achieve and what it will take until graduation to make it happen.

WHEN DO YOU START TRANSITION PLANNING?

It is never too early to start planning. The general rule is around fourteen. The age varies from state to state but must be started at the time" the child turns sixteen.

Remember when you begin planning to have a backup plan. At times it pays to have more than one backup plan.

Some parents begin planning during the middle school years. It depends on your situation because sometimes it can take a long time to reach certain goals.

WHO IS INVOLVED IN THE PLANNING PROCESS?

Your child is the most important member of the team. WHY? It is because it is his or her life that you are planning. Try to have your child attend the meetings. The earlier that this takes place the better. Help your child take a proactive role in the future. There is a saying "nothing about me, without me".

Parents, grandparents, relatives and friends are important members of the planning process. They have valuable information about your child to contribute to the planning process.

The school system plays a major role in transition planning. This is the group of people who will be helping your child achieve the transition goals.

Program and service organizations that will be providing services for your child after high school should be involved in the planning process.

WHEN WILL THE TRANSITION PLAN BE COMPLETED?

The plan will never be completely finished. It will evolve into a different type of planning. The process never stops. Once your child has graduated you will have preparation for adult life with service providers.

Service organizations will be involved in the planning process after the schools have completed their role in your child's life. Once the transition plan is completed another process begins.

WHAT ISSUES WILL MY CHILD FACE AS THEY ENTER ADULTHOOD?

The first issue that your child will face will be qualifying for services. Your child will no longer be entitled to services. He or she must qualify for all services received.

Living arrangements are a major issue as your child enters adulthood. Where will my child live? At home with family, in an apartment or home of their own, with friends in supported living or in a group home. You will need to think about this long before high school is completed because many places have waiting lists.

Transportation is an important issue in adulthood. This is especially true if the individual has a job. Many young adults with disabilities do not drive and must depend on other sources for their transportation needs. Family and friends can be a good source for providing transportation. Depending on where you live, public transportation may be a good resource for transportation. If none of these options are available, there are organizations that provide transportation to the disabled and elderly.

Socialization plays an important role in the lives of people with disabilities. Now that school has ended, you will need to find avenues for your young adult to be with his or her peers. Many organizations offer opportunities for socialization. A few examples are the local ARC and Special Olympics. Many churches also offer special classes and events for individuals to have interaction with their peers.

Working is a major step into adulthood. What type of work will your young adult be doing? You should begin to explore the job avenues during the transition process. The school system should help your child to explore their talents. It is important to take into consideration your child's strengths, weaknesses, likes and dislikes before seeking employment. This will help service providers in their search for the best employment solution for your young adult.

There are service providers that offer supported employment for individuals with disabilities. They will help teach your young adult the skills needed to be successful in the work place.

Many parents worry that if their child works he or she will lose social security benefits. This is not true. Many of the individuals can make more money and keep most of their benefits including monies provided by social security. There are benefit specialist that can help families look at the options and calculate the amount of benefits that can be retained when an individual goes to work.

Adult issues are dramatically different from those faced during the educational years. Services and programs are no longer an entitlement. The individual must qualify for each and every service. It is never too early to start exploring what types of services your young adult will be able to qualify for after high school. Many services and programs come complete with waiting lists. It is better to do your research than to suddenly find out that needed services can no longer be provided one the educational years have ended.

RETIREMENT YEARS

Aging is a natural part of life. As parents begin to get older and head towards the golden years, the children are also getting older. Parents always worry about their children's futures but there are added concerns when the children have disabilities. The biggest concern seems to be the care of the child after the parent is gone.

WHO WILL TAKE CARE OF MY CHILD WHEN I AM NO LONGER ABLE?

Planning is the key to making sure that your adult child will be taking care of. It is not something that can be taken care of in the spur of the moment. You need to consider all of the options that are available. Generally if no planning has been done, the state will take over the care of your child.

Do you have a conservatorship for your child? Have you named someone to take your place in the event that you are unable to continue as the conservator? Talk to your lawyer. Discuss the best options.

Learn about special needs trusts and how they can benefit your child. Look into the options of a microboard. They are non-profit companies set up by family members to provide services for your child.

Many aging individuals with disabilities end up in a group or nursing home setting. Because the individual cannot care for themselves, there may not be any options.

Have a family meeting and find out if any family members will be willing to take on the responsibility of care for your child after you are no longer able.

HOW DO I BEGIN THE PLANNING PROCESS?

Arrange to have a meeting with your child's case manager and discuss what options will be available to your child as he or she ages.

Contact your local ARC and hold a PATH for your child. Bring in individuals from your family and community to discuss the type of life that you wish for your child. PATH is a process to help determine strategies to overcome complex problems. It is a several step process that will help families network with individuals that can help with the complex issues.

Talk to your child and find out what his or her wishes are for the future.

Bring your family together and talk about your child's future.

ARE THERE ORGANIZATIONS THAT WILL HELP ARE FOR MY CHILD AFTER I AM GONE?

Yes. There are organizations that will provide care and services for your child as they grow older. Contact the Department of Aging in your area to find out what is available.

Many individuals will be receiving services from Medicaid Waiver Services at this time. The state and federal agencies will be overseeing the wavier programs.

Friends and family may offer options for the continued care of your child.

Both parents and children will grow older. There will be a time in the future when aging parents are no longer capable of caring for the children. Planning for the inevitability will be a most important component in your child's future. You and your child may both be young but the reality is that strategies need to be put in place for the future.

NATIONAL RESOURCES

Here is a small list of organizations that will get you started in finding the services needed by your family. Don't be afraid to contact them because they are there to help families just like yours.

ARC" The Arc of the United States
1010 Wayne Avenue, Suite 650
Silver Spring, MD 20910
Phone: (301) 565-3842 / (800) 433-5255
Fax: (301) 565-3843 / (301) 565-5342
www.thearc.org

ASSOCIATION FOR PERSONS
WITH SEVERE HANDICAPS" (TASH)
1025 Vermont Avenue Suite 300
Washington, DC 20005
(202)540-9020
www.tash.org

NATIONAL INFORMATION CENTER FOR CHILDREN
AND YOUTH WITH DISABILITIES" (NIHCY)
1825 Connecticut Ave NW, Suite 700
Washington, DC 20009
(800)695-0285 (Voice/TTY)
www.nichy.org

NATIONAL EASTER SEALS SOCIETY
233 S. Wacker Drive Suite 2400
Chicago, IL 60606
(800)221-6827
www.easterseals.com

NATIONAL ALLIANCE FOR" THE MENTALLY ILL"
(NAMI)
2107 Wilson Blvd, 300
Arlington, VA 22201
(800)950-6264
www.nami.org

NATIONAL COUNCIL ON DISABILITIES
1331 F Street Ste 850
Washington, DC 20004
(202)272-2004
www.ncd.gov

NATIONAL ORGRANIZATIONS FOR RARE DISORDERS
(NORD)
55 Kenosia Avenue
PO Box 1968Danbury, CT 06813-1968
(203) 744-0100
www.rarediseases.org

OFFICE OF SPECIAL PROGRAMS (OSEP)
Office of Special Education Programs
Office of Special Education and Rehabilitative Services
U.S. Department of Education
400 Maryland Ave., S.W.
Washington, DC 20202-7100
(202) 245-7459
www.edu.gov/about/offices/list/osers/osep/index.html

SOCIAL SECURITY ADMINISTRATION
Office of Public Inquiries
Windsor Park Building
6401 Security Blvd.
Baltimore, MD 21235 (800)772-1213
www.ssa.org

STATE RESOURCES

The following lists of resources are ones that I have used in Tennessee and Texas along Rachael's journey.

TENNESSEE RESOURCES:
CEREBRAL PALSY CENTER OF KNOXVILLE
241 E. Woodland Avenue
Knoxville, Tennessee 37917
(865) 523-0491
www.cpcenter.org

EAST TN TECHNOLOGY ACCESS CENTER
4918 North Broadway
Knoxville, TN 37918"
(865) 219-0130 (voice/TTY)
http://www.korrnet.org/ettac

SUPPORT AND TRAINING FOR EXCEPTIONAL
PARENTS" (STEP)
712 Professional Plaza
Greenville, TN 37745
(800)280-STEP
www.tnstep.org

TENNESSEE DEPARTMENT OF MENTAL HEALTH
& DELEVOPMENT DISABILITIES
Central Office
425 Fifth Avenue North
3rd Floor Cordell Hull Bldg
Nashville, Tennessee 37243-0675
(615) 532-6500
www.state.tn.us/mental/

TEXAS RESOURCES:
CENTRAL COUNTY CENTERS FOR MHMR SERVICES
304 South 22nd Street
Temple, TX 76501
(254) 298-7000
www.cccmhmr.com

CHILDREN'S SPECIAL NEEDS NETWORK
Heart of Central Texas Independent Living Center
222 East Central Avenue
Belton, Texas 76513
(800)300-6940
www.special-children.org

DEPARTMENT OF ASSISTIVE AND
REHABILATATIVE SERVICES" (DARS)
4800 N. Lamar Blvd.
Austin, Texas 78756
(800)628-5115
www.dars.state.tx.ys

PARTNERS RESOURCE NETWORK
1090 Longfellow Drive, Suite B
Beaumont, TX 77706
(409)898-4684
www.partnerstx.org

THE TEXAS DEPARTMENT OF AGING AND
DISABILITY SERVICES (DADS)
701 W. 51st St.
Austin, Texas 78751
512-438-3011
www.dads.state.tx.us

For speaking engagements, consultations or more information, contact the author at:

d.flanery@dflanery.com